In *December's Song,* Marilyn Heavilin addresses difficult issues such as multiple loss, suicide, AIDS, and the sovereignty of God, with the sensitivity and discernment that has come from her own life-and-death experiences. Pastors and laity alike will benefit from her practical approach to meeting the needs of hurting people.

Jim McClellan, Pastor
Host, JOY, TBN

December's Song is a melodious score written for bereaved singers confronted with the dissonant chords of grief. Marilyn Heavilin has opened her heart . . . broken by the death of her three sons . . . to pour out a sweet song of hope and encouragement to others who face the confusing noisy music of a loved one's death.

It is a classic piece for anyone who has loved, and for everyone who cares.

Jan Silvious, Co-Host
HOPE FOR THE HEART

While medical students are generally taught how to deal with a patient who is terminally ill, few receive training in how to help the bereaved family. In *December's Song,* Marilyn Heavilin gives precise suggestions on how to effectively meet the needs of the family as well as those of the patient. All professional caregivers will benefit from this sensitive and insightful book.

Charles M. Maples, M.D.
Diplomat of American Board of
Family Practice

Other Books by Marilyn Heavilin

Roses in December
Mother to Daughter: Becoming a Woman of Honor

Available from your local Christian bookstore
or
Here's Life Publishers.

December's Song

Marilyn Willett Heavilin

Here's Life Publishers

First printing, July 1988
Second printing, September 1989

Published by
HERE'S LIFE PUBLISHERS, INC.
P. O. Box 1576
San Bernardino, CA 92402

Library of Congress Cataloging-in-Publication Data
    Heavilin, Marilyn Willett.
       December's song : handling the realities of grief / Marilyn Willett
Heavilin
      p.   cm.
      ISBN 0-89840-210-7 (pbk.)
      1. Grief. 2. Bereavement—Psychological aspects. 3. Death—
Psychological aspects. 4. Consolation. 5. Heavilin, Marilyn Willett.
6. Christian biography—United States. I. Title.
      BF575.G7H42   1988   88-789
      155.9'37—dc 19   CIP

Unless otherwise indicated, Scripture quotations are from the *King James
Version.*
    Scripture quotations designated NIV are from *The Holy Bible, New Interna-
tional Version,* © 1978 by the New York International Bible Society, published
by the Zondervan Corporation, Grand Rapids, Michigan.
    Scripture quotations designated TLB are from *The Living Bible,* © 1971 by
Tyndale House Publishers, Wheaton, Illinois.
    Scripture quotations designated NASB are from *The New American Stan-
dard Bible,* © The Lockman Foundation 1960, 1962, 1963, 1968, 1971, 1972,
1975, 1977.

Cover song, *Pierce My Ear.* Words and music by Steve Croft.
© 1980 by Dayspring Music (a div. of WORD, Inc.)
All rights reserved. International copyright secured. Used by permission.

For More Information, Write:
L.I.F.E.—P.O. Box A399, Sydney South 2000, Australia
Campus Crusade for Christ of Canada—Box 300, Vancouver, B.C., V6C 2X3, Canada
Campus Crusade for Christ—Pearl Assurance House, 4 Temple Row, Birmingham, B2 5HG, England
Lay Institute for Evangelism—P.O. Box 8786, Auckland 3, New Zealand
Campus Crusade for Christ—P.O. Box 240, Colombo Court Post Office, Singapore 9117
Great Commission Movement of Nigeria—P.O. Box 500, Jos, Plateau State Nigeria, West Africa
Campus Crusade for Christ International—Arrowhead Springs, San Bernardino, CA 92414, U.S.A.

to

Katherine Naté

our precious new rose

who has put
a new song
in our hearts

Contents

THE HEALER

Acknowledgments

With Heartfelt Thanks

To the bereaved families who willingly shared their pain and sorrow with me so that I might pass their observations and experiences on to other hurting families.

To Les Stobbe, Wayne Hastings, Dan Benson, Jean Bryant, and the rest of the Here's Life staff who are a constant encouragement to me.

To the participants in the Inland Empire chapter of The Compassionate Friends who have been a sounding board for many of my ideas.

To the Reverend Tom Burris and the Reverend Earle Rosenberger for their patience as they read my material and endeavored to answer my theological questions.

To my family who once again gave me room to share some of our most private experiences so that others might learn how to live through the death of a loved one.

THE HURTING

I weep with grief;
my heart is heavy with sorrow;
encourage and cheer me
with your words
(Psalm 119:28, TLB).

A Familiar Song

---

*Surviving when death or disaster visits
again and again*

It was a quiet Saturday morning. I was just finishing
my Bible reading and slowly sipping a cup of tea when the
phone rang and abruptly ended my reverie.

"The baby's coming!" announced the voice on the other
end of the telephone line. I hurried upstairs to tell my husband Glen, "You're going to be a grandpa today!"

Glen and I hurried to get dressed. We gathered up a few
personal items in case we had to stay overnight, and we
were soon on our way.

During the two-hour drive to our son's town, we silently prayed for our daughter-in-law Debbie and for Matt.
Occasionally we talked about the changes that were coming. We were going to be grandparents. What fun!

As we walked into the hospital, Glen proudly asked
directions to the maternity waiting room and we were
directed to the fourth floor. As we stepped off the elevator,
we paused for a moment trying to figure which way to turn,
and a young man from our son's church walked up to us.

"Mr. and Mrs. Heavilin, I'm here to take you to Matt.
The baby has been born but there were some complications

13

in delivery. Matt is in ICU watching the doctors. They're working with the baby because they're not sure she'll live."

A multitude of thoughts and questions raced through my mind:

Our grandbaby is here — a little girl.

Complications — what kind of complications?

How could anything go wrong? Debbie is so healthy. She took such good care of herself during the pregnancy. She didn't take medication, and she wouldn't even drink coffee or tea!

The baby might not live? Impossible. Absolutely impossible. This couldn't be happening to us again — please, dear Lord, not again...

When we turned the corner, I saw Matt explaining the situation to Debbie's parents who also had just arrived.

Matt came to me and hugged me tightly. We couldn't speak, but our eyes communicated everything we were thinking and feeling. We'd been through this before.

Earlier Pain

When Matt was five and his sister Mellyn was three, our third child, Jimmy, was born. When Jimmy was seven weeks old, Glen walked into his room early one morning and discovered he had died of crib death during the night.

As we waited for the coroner that day, I scooped Matt and Mellyn up in my arms and took them to my next door neighbor's home, trying to explain to them that Jimmy was now in heaven.

We had barely grown accustomed to our grief when, a year and a half later, our identical twin boys, Nathan and Ethan, were born on Christmas morning.

My parents brought Matt and Mellyn to the hospital on Christmas afternoon. Although they were not allowed to visit me, my room was on the ground floor, and we arranged to have the twins in my room so that Matt and Mellyn could view them through the window.

I can still see their hopeful little faces pressed against the window. Surely our pain from Jimmy's death would go away now that they had two brothers.

We brought Nathan home on New Year's Eve, but Ethan needed to gain more weight before he could be released.

I visited Ethan each day, and I saw that he was not gaining weight; in fact, he was losing. Soon my greatest fears were confirmed: Ethan had pneumonia. The doctors worked hard to save him, but he died when he was ten days old.

I had to tell my children that another brother had left them and was now in heaven. My dear Matt who had proudly taken pictures of his twin brothers to school for his classmates to see now had to tell them that one of his little brothers had died.

I remember thinking then, *Little children shouldn't have to deal with the fact that babies can die.* I wish no one, not even adults, had to deal with such terrible heartbreaks.

Our family slowly regained its equilibrium, and the children grew up. Matt and Mellyn graduated from high school and went on to college. Mellyn married, and Nate became a junior in high school. Then once again we were hit by a death blow—Nate was killed in a car crash caused by a drinking driver.

It had happened again. That familiar song began to ring in my ears, and it was bitterly painful.

The only thing worse for me than my own grief was the pain I felt as I watched my two remaining children suffer the death of yet another brother.

I feel Matt suffered the greatest personal loss. One day,

through his tears, he said to me, "Mellyn has her husband to help her through this, and you and Daddy have each other, but I don't have anybody because Nate was my best friend — and now he's dead."

Matt, along with the rest of the family, has worked through much of his grief since that time. Shortly after Nathan's death, I shared with some friends that I dreaded Christmas because it was Nate's birthday. I had commented, "I would like to ask God to cancel December. We'll try it again some other year."

The next day while browsing in a bookstore, I discovered a poster of a beautiful red rose, but what really caught my attention was the statement at the bottom of the poster:

GOD GIVES US MEMORIES SO WE MIGHT HAVE

ROSES IN DECEMBER.[1]

Through the years we have collected some very special roses — in actual flowers, in friends, and in memories.

One of our most treasured roses is our daughter-in-law Debbie, one of Nate's best friends. She and Matt were married about two years after Nate's death.

Grief on Top of Grief

When Matt and Debbie announced that a baby was coming, we were all excited. This baby was going to be a very special rose in our lives. Then as I stood with Matt and watched the doctors work over my little grandbaby, in my heart I cried, *Lord, this song is too familiar. We want to sing a new song, a song of spring, of joy. I thought we were beyond December. How can this be happening again?*

I am not the only one who has asked that question. In the first few weeks after Nathan's death, I felt sure that no other parents had experienced the deaths of three of their children. Yet when I emerged from my own cocoon of grief long enough to observe others around me, I discovered I had a lot of company.

At a workshop I presented on "Multiple Loss," Angie told of the sudden death of her stepson Jeffrey to leukemia in 1975 — only thirty-six hours after the disease was diagnosed. Five years later, in separate accidents within a period of less than four months, her two sons Anthony and André were killed by drinking drivers. Today I received a letter from Angie giving me permission to share her story. She told me that her husband lost his battle with cancer and died just two weeks ago.

Many parents have experienced the sequential deaths of two or more of their children, and others have encountered the simultaneous deaths of children and a spouse or other family member. At a recent national convention of The Compassionate Friends,[2] Ron related how his sister, her husband, their three children and Ron's two children all died in the same car crash. Frequently, as in Ron's case, these tragedies claim all the children in a family.

I've heard people make comments such as, "Grief is grief; it probably isn't much different when more than one person dies. It may take a little longer to work through it, but at least they've had experience in these things, so it'll probably be easier this time."

Before Nathan died, I would have been inclined to agree with that thought. I really believed that, since we already had experienced the deaths of two children and knew the pain we would be facing, perhaps we could work through it more quickly this time. Maybe it wouldn't hurt quite so much.

How little I knew!

While it was true that through Jimmy and Ethan's deaths I had discovered God's faithfulness in providing His strength and power to enable me to survive these devastating traumas, one grief experience compounded the next one, and I was dealing with grief on top of grief.

Happily, with our granddaughter, although she came very near to death, God saw fit to spare her life. However, I am observing that our family is reacting to even the threat of death in a much more dramatic and intense way than those who have never faced death before. Glen and I experienced the symptoms of grief all over again: sleepless nights, depression, fear, restlessness, lack of concentration, and even anger. December's song comes easily for us. Our granddaughter is recovering and developing beautifully, but we are singing the song of joy guardedly.

Since the release of my first book, *Roses in December*,[3] in February 1987, I have had the opportunity to talk with and read letters from hundreds of families who are experiencing grief. My friend Colleen's letter is an example:

> *My losses haven't all been deaths, but disappointments, too, all very close together. The year my husband and I were married, I was diagnosed with a type of rheumatoid arthritis. Two years later I miscarried. One year later Sarah was born (one good point!). Two and a half years after Sarah, Jasmine was born with Down's Syndrome — a disappointment, but we were praising God for a healthy heart. At six months her "healthy" heart failed and she died. Due to her death, problems developed with our medical insurance. Our business was going under, and we were put on payments with the IRS. A year later my grandma, whom I loved dearly and was very close to, died while I was talking with her. Soon after that I was in a car accident that almost took my life, did take a one-year recovery, and put our finally balancing finances back in turmoil.*
>
> *After all this my feelings are just to do my best and keep looking up through all these difficulties. My husband on the other hand goes through deep bouts of depression. "Why do all these things keep happening to us? Why do other people prosper, and they don't seem to care about us or realize their good fortune?"*
>
> *I often wonder what's around the corner for us, and*

I live in fear. What could happen next? I think these problems build one upon another. If any one of these things had happened, that would be somewhat understandable, but they all happened in a few short years.

A friend with a very easy life and deep dedication to God and His service told me she often wonders if God loves her because everybody seems to have trials except her family! I don't know what that is supposed to mean; it's confusing to me.

The conclusion I have come to with multiple griefs is that after awhile our thinking becomes a little warped; sometimes we allow ourselves to just keep existing and never really live. We often become very pessimistic about everything. Even Christians begin to doubt the very foundation of their faith. I think a lot of these issues are decisions of the soul only to be wrestled through with God over a period of time. Maybe, if we can continue to trust our faith and go on from fact rather than feelings, things will balance out and the feelings will slowly return.

As I talk with grieving people, I find that several topics keep coming up:

- How can we keep our marriage together?
- I can't get rid of this deep depression.
- How can we face it if it happens again?
- How can we deal with the hindrances to healing?
- Our loved one committed suicide [had AIDS, or was the victim of a violent crime] — how do we deal with it?
- We're faced with legal complications concerning the death — what do we do?
- Why don't professional caregivers know how to work with us?
- Where does God fit into all of this?

If you have experienced a severe traumatic loss, or a multiple loss in your life, or some of the other special circumstances mentioned above, perhaps you feel you have been living in December, that wintertime of your life, much too long. December's song of grief is droning on and on in your mind.

I have good news for you. The song of grief is not the only December song there is. Come with me as we discover and sing the various other songs of December, the songs of the bereaved and the songs other people can sing to us. Then we'll move beyond December's grief music to a new, brighter, more pleasant melody.

A Song of Strength

---

*Handling the stress on marriage, siblings,
health, careers, and holiday celebrations*

When someone dies, the surviving family will be subject to various stresses. In this chapter I am going to highlight those stresses which have been mentioned to me most often as I have talked with grieving families.

Marriage

The Compassionate Friends organization reports that approximately 75 percent of the couples who lose one child divorce within the first five years after the death of their child. With each death or additional trauma, the marital stress is likely to increase. Often couples can weather the storm of one tragedy, but their resistance wears down as the second or third trauma occurs. They simply get tired and don't have the energy it takes to fend off the resulting emotions or to resist temptations which may come after repeated painful experiences.

Glen and I weathered the deaths of Jimmy and Ethan without being particularly aware, at the time, of the effect on our marriage. As I look back, though, I realize we both went through many unusually difficult times. It just didn't dawn on us that the cause of our troubles could be the deaths of our children.

When Nathan was killed seventeen years later, Glen and I had many disagreements and we couldn't communicate much of anything except, "I don't like the way you're handling this. You're different from the way you used to be." This time it was easy to figure out what was causing our problems, but we still didn't know what to do about them.

We never discussed divorce, but there were days when we each wished the other wouldn't come home. Everything seemed quite peaceful as long as we didn't have to talk to each other and didn't have to agree on anything.

Differences

We all hope to find security in having others think the same and react the same as we do, but God did not make us all alike and we seldom marry someone with the same strengths and weaknesses we possess.

As the stress was building between Glen and me after Nathan's death, I had the opportunity to take a Personality Profile test, presented by Florence Littauer in her book, *Personality Plus.* She presents the four basic temperaments (personality types) as Sanguine, Choleric, Melancholy, and Phlegmatic. She also states that most of us will have a primary and a secondary temperament. According to Florence, each temperament comes equipped with a basic goal: The Sanguine wants to have *fun;* the Choleric needs *control;* the Melancholy strives for *perfection;* and the Phlegmatic desires *peace.*[1]

The Sanguine will continue to try to find fun even in the midst of his grief. He may display superficial joy and try to make people laugh, even at the funeral. While others in the family are crying and openly talking about their grief, the Sanguine may crack jokes that seem in poor taste in an effort to conjure up some fun and frivolity. The Sanguine has a very strong denial system and will seldom let you see the pain that may be behind his happy face. When asked how he is doing, he'll most likely respond, "Great, just great."

The Choleric will have little time for grief. He will begin to figure ways he can once again get control of his life. He may say something like, "It's over — let's get on with life." He will make quick changes (such as cleaning out the deceased person's room immediately or moving to a new house). The Choleric is afraid to show much emotion because it makes him vulnerable, causing him to feel that he's losing control. He will tend to harbor much anger toward God because he feels God has snatched the control of his life right out of his hands. The Choleric has the strongest denial system of all of the temperaments — he most likely will bury himself in work or some other activity to help him forget what has happened.

The Melancholy may be overwhelmed with guilt even if he had nothing to do with the person's death. He will have difficulty letting go of the person. The Melancholy will generally have the hardest time cleaning out the room of the deceased and packing away his possessions. If the death has occurred as the result of a violent crime, the Melancholy can easily work himself into a rage because of the injustice of the situation. If the case is not resolved properly, the Melancholy may go into a very deep depression that can last for months — or years.

The Phlegmatic feels things very deeply but has difficulty showing emotion outwardly or expressing his feelings verbally. During an emotional crisis he may become extremely withdrawn and critical, and his normally dry sense of humor may become very caustic.

As I marked my strengths and weaknesses on the personality profile, I observed they were quite opposite from Glen's. I began to understand why we were grieving so differently. My primary temperament is Melancholy with Choleric as my secondary. That means my basic goals are perfection and control. Glen's temperament is Phlegmatic with a touch of Sanguine. He wants peace with a little fun thrown in along the way.

No wonder there was stress in our marriage! Our son was dead; we were in the midst of a manslaughter case; the insurance settlement was taking too long. My life was out of control and nothing was perfect. From Glen's point of view, with all of these problems, peace was impossible and fun was out of the question. Our lives had been turned upside down.

As we realized we were grieving differently and had individual needs, we took some active steps to resolve the stress in our marriage.

First, we made a verbal commitment to each other and to God that we wanted our marriage to survive.

Second, we set aside some time where we could give our undivided attention to each other.

Then we asked each other, "What is the best thing I can do for you that would help you work through your own grief process?"

I said, "I have to keep talking until I'm all talked out. I want to control the manslaughter case and the insurance problems, but there doesn't seem to be anything I can do, so I just have to talk out my feelings and frustrations."

Glen replied, "When you keep talking and talking, I feel like you expect me to do something, and in this situation there's nothing I can do. Then I feel so helpless—like I'm letting you down, not meeting your needs."

It had been our policy to keep our troubles within the four walls of our home—I always shared my problems with Glen and only Glen. Now that pattern was putting undue pressure on us and on our marriage. Because Glen recognized I had to talk to someone, he gave me permission to share my stress with a few of our very close and trusted friends.

Glen shared that his greatest need was for frequent times of peace and quiet. I didn't feel so bad about going out with one of my friends when I realized that my chance to talk with a friend was also providing Glen with his much needed peace and quiet. I also learned to give him the freedom to sit quietly alone in our bedroom when I discovered it didn't mean he was mad at me or disapproving of something I had done; he just needed times of solitude.

An understanding of personality differences can help most any marriage. Two weeks after the release of *Roses in December,* I received a tape-letter from a woman named Mary Lou. She and her husband had been married over thirty years. They had one son who was stricken with multiple sclerosis which resulted in the end of his marriage and his inability to pass the bar exam even though he successfully completed law school. Another son died at twenty-two in a single-car crash, and Mary Lou's daughter was faced with a custody battle after a difficult divorce. The day Mary Lou made the tape for me, she and her husband had just returned from placing his mother in a convalescent home. She said:

> *Through all of these problems, our own marriage has remained quite stable, but last week my husband and I had a very strong verbal fight. We had never fought like that before, and it scared us. We wondered, "What's wrong with us? Is our marriage falling apart?"*
>
> *Then your book arrived and I read your chapter on "The Rose of Uniqueness." What an eye-opener. When I read it to my husband, he said, "Who is this lady? How does she know what's going on in our house?"*
>
> *You described our temperaments to a T, and now we are better equipped to give each other room to grieve.*

The Empty Nest

Further stresses within the grief process may be caused

by the unique circumstances within the family. If the deceased was an only child or the last child in the family, the family will have additional adjustments.

One mother whose youngest daughter died wrote to me:

No more parenting. She was the only child we were still parenting. Now I feel so much older . . . a "senior citizen," which I really am, but she kept us younger. No more trips to the college campus, no more Parents' Day each fall, no more Mother-Daughter Teas in the spring. No more hugs, no more long talks, no more shopping together or sitting across the table from each other . . . at family birthdays and Christmas she's always missing now. We feel sad that life goes on just as if she never existed.

Another mother, whose only child had been murdered, wrote:

I felt anger because my son was killed and people with large families had nothing happen. I felt it was very unfair.

After both of his children were killed in a car crash, Ron observed:

I'm no longer a father like other fathers. Social life has decreased a little and has changed in nature a lot because we no longer have children to do things together with as a family like we did before. Seeing my wife suffer from the loss has been almost unbearable.

Parents who lose all their children, or whose only child has died, must deal with the fact that they will never have grandchildren, and there will be no child to care for them in their old age. This is another adjustment that will be especially difficult.

Siblings

Stress on surviving siblings is intense when one child dies, but will multiply if the family loses more than one child. The remaining children may feel they have to fill the shoes of each of the deceased children. Our Matt commented after Nathan's death, "Do you know how it feels to have had three brothers and yet be the only one who can carry on the Heavilin name?" None of us had deliberately placed that pressure on him, but it was a fact we all had to face: If we were to have grandchildren who would carry on the Heavilin name, it was up to Matt.

The remaining children can also be hurt very deeply if they perceive that the deceased children were the favored ones, especially bright, unusually handsome, more fun, or ones the parents always depended on. The other children often feel guilty because they weren't the ones who died. My friend Joe saw his mother and his sister die of a hereditary problem within a year. Just a few months later, when Joe was told his brother Jack had died of the same disease, he fell to the floor, pounding his fists on the carpet, saying, "Why couldn't it have been me? Dad needs Jack because he loved him more. Why couldn't it have been me?" I'm sure Joe's father didn't mean to communicate to Joe that he was loved any less than Jack, but because of his feelings, Joe felt an added stress and undeserved guilt—he was still alive while the "important" members of the family were gone.

I met Alice at a state convention. She thanked me for talking about dealing with grief, and she shared that her brother had died when she was a teenager.

When I asked how her parents had dealt with his death, she said, "Oh, they never have dealt with it. Everything changed when my brother died. He was the 'perfect' one, and I've always felt my parents would have been better off if I had died instead of my brother."

Health

The increased stress of trauma can have a devastating impact on the family's health. After our seven-week-old Jimmy died, my health went downhill and I had two major surgeries within the next year. Within seven weeks of Ethan's death I had to have a total hysterectomy, and six

months after Nathan's death I was in the hospital with
pneumonia.

A sudden traumatic death in a family can even be followed quickly by a terminal illness of at least one other
family member, especially if the family is not allowing
themselves to grieve properly.

William R. Dubin, M.D., said in his article "Sudden Unexpected Death: Intervention With the Survivors":

> When sudden unexpected death occurs, a significant
> and meaningful relationship has been lost without warn-
> ing. The abrupt transition from life to death shocks even
> professional observers, let alone those whose lives will be
> seriously changed. Unexpected and untimely deaths are
> conspicuous because the person is not only active and
> visible at the time of death, but is a significant force in
> the lives of the survivors.
>
> The grieving process may begin in the ER [hospital
> emergency room] after the survivors are informed of
> their loss. The initial contact with the survivors will have
> a significant impact on their grief response. Inadvertent
> inhibition of this process can result in a pathological
> response with an increased risk of morbidity and/or mor-
> tality.[2]

Dr. Edgar N. Jackson stated in an interview:

> Acute grief can cause death if it is not managed cor-
> rectly.
>
> Within a year after the death of their husbands, wid-
> ows in Cambridge, Massachusetts, died at several times
> the rate of other women their age, a study found.
>
> Within eighteen months after a woman divorced her
> husband, her son, deeply attached to his father, died of
> lymphatic leukemia.
>
> The severity of the results of untreated grief—among
> them, vandalism and physical and mental illness—make
> it imperative that somebody help the grieving to work
> through their grief.[3]

Sometimes death following a loss happens because of
the extreme emotional and physical stress caused by the
loss; other times the beleaguered family just doesn't have

the will to fight anymore. When I was in the hospital with pneumonia, six months after Nathan's death, I felt that way. One evening my temperature was very high and I had not been able to keep any food down in three days. I recall thinking, *If this medication doesn't take hold pretty soon, I could die.* The thought didn't upset me at all. I just rolled over and reasoned, *Fine. I have more children in heaven than I have here, so it's OK with me if I die.* I was too tired to fight.

Often when a middle-aged child dies and his elderly parents survive, I've heard the parents comment, "Why couldn't it have been me? He was too young to die. Now I don't want to live." It is important that friends and family stay close to the bereaved and try to give them reasons for living.

Career

After several traumas, it is very common for a person to lose sight of career goals. Men, who are usually the major breadwinners in a family, have an especially difficult time allowing themselves to grieve while continuing in their professions. Paul told me, "Before my two children died, my job was really important to me. I used to enjoy my work, but now I go to work and realize it doesn't matter anymore. I can't concentrate on my assignments and I really don't care."

Another parent said, "I used to be driven toward financial success, but now I make just enough money to live on. I don't have the energy to do any more. I just can't stand the stress."

In our society working men and women unfortunately are not really allowed to grieve. They are given three or four days bereavement leave, and that's it. They are then expected to go back to work and perform normally. Obviously these people feel the pressure of meeting family and work responsibilities: *The house payment has to be made;*

Billy still needs braces; we're counting on my income for Cathy's college tuition; that work project deadline must be met; I have an important report to give on Friday. There's no time to grieve.

Two years before Nate died, I graduated from college and started working as the academic counselor at the high school Nate attended. The year he died, I was teaching an English literature class — something I had always wanted to do. I loved my job and intended to continue in that career for many years.

After Nate died, I dreaded going to work each day, and preparing for my classes became drudgery. I lost interest in my "dream" job — it didn't matter anymore.

Holidays

Another stress area will be the holidays. Families may need to give themselves permission not to celebrate holidays in the same way they did before their loved one died. After the death of their eighteen-year-old daughter, one family I knew went on a picnic for Thanksgiving and took a trip over the Christmas holidays. It is important for the family to talk together and be allowed to express their feelings freely about upcoming seasonal holidays, birthdays and anniversaries.

If this is the case in your family, don't be hard on yourselves. The world is not going to stop if you don't celebrate Christmas this year. Some of your extended family may feel frustrated, but try to explain as kindly and gently as you can that your heart is just not ready for big celebrations yet.

This can be a time to make some new memories and establish new traditions. It was four years after Nathan's death before I could do much Christmas decorating or have a real tree. Last year, though, Glen and I went out and cut down the biggest tree we could find. Since we had recently bought and refurbished a seventy-five-year-old Victorian house, I made many new decorations for our Christmas tree and did everything I could think of to use the Victorian theme all through the holidays.

To celebrate, Glen and I invited friends to go Christmas caroling with us. Several women friends joined me one afternoon for a Victorian tea and a brief piano and violin recital provided by one of my friends. These events took planning and effort on my part, and it wasn't always easy. Yet as we build new memories, we will become more confident that we can face the holidays and the future without our loved one.

Often after the death of a child or spouse, adults would be quite content to ignore the holidays, but they are forced to face traditional celebrations because of other children in the family. Friends can help in these situations by offering to take the children Christmas shopping, or to visit Santa Claus.

One family told me how they spent their first Christmas afternoon assembling a memory book of their deceased child. There were tears, of course, but they also spent a lot of time laughing as the pictures and notes brought back thoughts of the wonderful times they had had together. A family activity like this can help the children approach grieving in a healthy way.

It is important also for us to be sensitive when choosing Christmas cards for the recently bereaved. I was so relieved when I opened one envelope and read a card which said, "To Comfort You at Christmas." What a contrast to all of the jolly, "Ho, Ho, Ho" cards that arrived in each day's mail. Your writing a note to the bereaved family acknowledging that this holiday may be difficult and perhaps including a positive statement or story about the deceased will be appreciated.

All of these problems following a loss will add tremendous stress to family relationships. However, our woeful song of stress can be transposed into a song of strength when we identify our stresses and reach for the help we need to face them.

A Song of Peace

Moving from depression and despair to peace and productivity

Often our December song becomes a song of despair and futility. There may be times when you get stuck in your grief work and can't seem to pull yourself out of that bottomless pit of hopelessness. Please realize it is all right to ask for help.

Bobbi came to one of my seminars in Boise, Idaho. Six months after her daughter's death, Bobbi was desperate. As she walked into her local bookstore, she silently prayed, "Lord, I'm certain I am going crazy, but I don't know where to turn. If there is a book here that can help me, please let me find it." As she approached the grief section, she noticed *Roses In December*. She read the back cover and thought, *Perhaps someone who has lost three children will be able to help me.* As she thumbed through the pages, she found the story where I called a friend and asked, "Do you think I'm still sane?" Then Bobbi knew this book was for her.

Each of us probably will reach a point in our grief work where we need help beyond ourselves. If you don't have a friend who can help you through this wintertime of grief, seek a professional. You may find it worth his fee just to know you have someone who will listen to you and help you work through your feelings.

Because of my melancholy temperament, I very easily slipped into deep depression after Nate's death . There were times I felt so overwhelmed I was unable to speak. I knew if I opened my mouth my pain would tumble out in uncontrollable sobs. Frequently when Glen would try to find out what was troubling me, I wrote him notes because I was afraid to try to talk:

> *I am not mad at you. I just can't talk right now. Please pray for me.*

Working Through the Problems

About this time, someone gave me *Blow Away the Black Clouds* by Florence Littauer. As I read it, I began to implement some of her suggestions for working through difficult times:

- Recognize the problem
- Decide you need help
- Examine the causes
- Look at the alternatives
- Check your health
- Analyze self-pity
- Avoid trouble[1]

Recognize the problem

The problem was . . .   my son was dead, and I had lost interest in living. Nothing really mattered anymore, and I couldn't conquer my depression.

Decide you need help

I knew I had little chance of working things out with Glen if I couldn't get my depression under control. As a Christian, I felt guilty because I wasn't able to get on top of my depression by myself. I felt sure God was disappointed in me because I wasn't able to rise above my problems alone, but I knew He would be even more upset with me if I stayed in the pits. I determined to get some help.

I forced myself to have a quiet time with the Lord each day, although at first it seemed nothing more than a ritual. I attended several motivational seminars, and I spent a day in prayer and counseling with Philippian Ministries.[2] I read every book I could find on dealing with grief and depression, and I made myself accountable to several friends who were willing to check my progress.

Examine the causes

The obvious cause of my depression was that my son was dead. The underlying cause was that I was angry at God, and really I guess I was simply mad at the whole world. Life wasn't fair, and I hated that fact. As I spent time in God's Word, and as I followed the counseling and reading program suggested by Philippian Ministries, I was able to resolve the anger and learn how to deal with it immediately when it appeared.

Look at the alternatives

1. I could stay mad and wallow in self-pity.

2. I could walk away from Glen, my family, my problems.

3. I could accept the fact Nate was dead and work at establishing a new normal pattern of living.

Once I acknowledged that Nate's death was not just a bad dream . . . it was not going to have a happy ending . . . Nate was not going to reappear and say, "I fooled you," I was able to pick up the pieces and move on. Some people can do that very quickly. It took me many months, but by then I was able to assess what was left of my life and determine to do something with it. That's when I started to prepare myself as a speaker. I felt perhaps somebody else could profit from my experiences — even my experiences of depression.

Check your health

After Nate's death, I did not sleep well and seldom got enough rest. At first I overworked myself in an attempt to block out reality. I finally wore myself down to the point where I contracted pneumonia and was in the hospital for six days. I was not in good health, but I really didn't care.

After I decided I wanted to recover from this nightmare, I enrolled in a nutrition, weight and exercise program. I now make sure I have regular health check-ups and both Glen and I have established a pattern of walking around our neighborhood often. Our schedule is very busy and hectic, but to keep the stress level down, we frequently take off to the beach in our motor home.

Analyze self-pity

After losing three sons, I was convinced that no one had ever suffered more than I had. Then I read Joni Eareckson Tada's book, *A Step Further.* Joni explains that when we are in the midst of suffering, whether it be a hangnail, a flat tire, unemployment, or the loss of a loved one, we each tend to feel we are at the top of the scale of suffering.[3] When I thought of Joni confined to a wheelchair for the rest of her life, having to depend on others to meet her every need, my problems paled in comparison. Once I was willing to look beyond myself, I realized there were many people in situations worse than mine.

Avoid trouble

One of the things that depressed me most about Nate's death was the long, drawn-out insurance problems and the manslaughter trial which was postponed eleven times. My son Matt observed that my depression increased when I received phone calls from the district attorney, the insurance company or the families whose children had been in the car with Nate but had survived the crash.

Matt bought me an answering machine, pointing out that I didn't need to answer the phone until after I heard who was calling. At first I insisted I had an "obligation" to answer my phone—it wasn't honest not to answer it if I was actually home. But finally Matt got through to me. I began to realize I was playing the martyr by insisting I answer the phone every time it rang, and I was flirting with depression. I learned to screen my calls and let Glen return some of them when he came home.

I gave myself permission not to attend every school function because each time I attended one, I came home depressed. I also released myself from the mandate to perform at 100 percent all of the time. Once I did that I was able to request, without feeling guilty, that my work assignment be reduced to part-time.

Doing things alone which Nate and I had done together before caused depression. Often in the morning I would start out for my work feeling pretty good, but by the time I had driven the twelve miles to the school alone, dwelling on how much fun the ride had been when Nate and I rode together, I would arrive in an emotional heap. Although I couldn't avoid the drive, I finally determined to channel my thoughts by listening to Christian messages and songs on tape. In the afternoon on the way home, I listened to "Talk From the Heart," a Christian radio talk show hosted by Rich Buhler. As I listened to that program, I began to realize that other people were hurting, too. I remember the day I mustered up enough nerve to call in to the show and offer advice to another grieving parent. I never dreamed then that someday I would be a guest on Rich's program and have an opportunity to help hundreds, perhaps even thousands, of hurting people.

As I reduced the stressful situations, forced myself to take preventative measures, and looked beyond my December to see others' pain, I became depressed less often.

Build Your Rock Pile

In the Bible, especially the Old Testament, whenever

something of historical importance happened, the people marked the event by erecting a pile of rocks as a reminder. As a positive step away from depression and toward peace, I would recommend that you construct a memorial, a figurative rock pile, to each one of your deceased loved ones. It may be a little journal that you have written about that person. If it's a stillborn child or a child who lived just a few days, then there won't be much that you can write about the child, but you can write about the pregnancy, or how the rest of the family was getting ready for this child, or even some funny little thing that happened during the birth. In our house our "rock pile" is a stained-glass window designed with one rose in full bloom and two small rosebuds. It's our memorial corner for our boys. That window serves as a daily reminder that these boys were a special part of our family.

You may find it helpful to write something you learned through knowing the person who died, whether you knew him just for a few minutes or for many years. Determine to become stronger in some area of your life because of that relationship.

When I look at my time with Jimmy, although I only had him for seven weeks, I know I became a better mother because of him. Through his death I realized how brief life could be, and I realized how precious my children are. I learned that we don't have a "right" to be a parent—it is a privilege. I know Jimmy's death altered my behavior with my own children and with other people's children.

Through Ethan's death I learned to be honest about my feelings. At first I was mad at God, and I told Him so. God and I talked it out several times. That was the first time I felt free to say, "God, it isn't fair. I'm mad. I think You've done us in." God didn't zap me. I didn't drop dead right there. God continued to love me and He didn't walk away from me. I began to realize that as long as I harbored anger and unforgiveness toward God or anyone else, I short-circuited the availability of God's power. As I learned to be honest with God, I learned I could be honest also with the people around me.

Because of Nathan's death, I have become much, much more sensitive to others and to their needs. I am better able to respond to others. I have determined that my boys' lives won't be wasted — I want them to count. I have to do it through me because they can't do it themselves, and I want everything that made their lives special to show through me. It mattered that they lived and it also mattered that they died. I am determined to make these experiences count in my life.

As we, the bereaved, acknowledge those things which are burdening us, admit that we need help beyond ourselves, deal with our depression step by step, and establish figurative rock piles to remind us of what we've learned, December's song of despair will become a song of peace.

THE HINDRANCES

Come quickly, Lord,
and answer me,
for my depression deepens;
don't turn away from me
or I shall die.
Let me see your kindness to me
in the morning,
for I am trusting you
(Psalm 143:7,8, TLB).

A Song of
Freedom

*Finding freedom from the fear that it will
happen again*

When someone dies, it is normal that we will fear, "It's going to happen again." When our seven-week-old Jimmy died, even our children feared another death. Several times I woke to the feel of a little hand moving across my face. As I stirred and opened my eyes, my three-year-old daughter would say, "I just wanted to see if God took you, too."

When life moves on for several years without any other major traumas, the fear of another death usually subsides. We may eventually feel safe again, but if another loss occurs, the fears return, and they will be increased.

In our case, death came again within a year and a half when our ten-day-old Ethan died of pneumonia. Instead of subsiding, my fears began to multiply. I remember many nights when I went into Nate's room and put my hand under his nose just to make sure he was still breathing. I had never done that with my older children.

Shortly after Ethan's death, I had to return to the hospital for major surgery and leave my little Nathan in someone else's care. After the surgery I became terribly ill. I could not keep any food down and I was losing strength and weight rapidly. After taking many tests, the doctor

43

realized my problem was not so much physical as it was emotional. He finally said, "Marilyn, I'm going to send you home to that baby and I think you'll be much better." He was right. Once I was able to hold Nate in my arms and reassure myself that he was all right, I began to eat and gain weight again.

Expecting the Worst

Our reaction to crises is different depending on our experiences with loss. When people who haven't experienced many traumas hear of an accident, they tend to think, *Oh, it probably isn't very serious. Everybody is going to be OK.* However, when those of us who have encountered multiple loss are informed of an accident, our first question tends to be, "Is he dead?"

After receiving word about Nate's accident, I called into Matt's bedroom, "There's been a terrible accident; we must hurry to the hospital." Matt recalls that even though his grandparents were gone that evening and they could have been the ones involved in the crash, he knew instinctively it was Nate. He also knew Nate was dying.

When I asked why he thought that, his answer showed the effect the earlier deaths of two brothers had had on him: "Heavilin kids don't come home from hospitals." Multiple traumas generate multiple fears.

I also find I have to be very careful when I'm around little babies. I worry if their fingers appear to be a little blue, their skin feels warm, they seem restless, or they sleep longer than usual. Generally the baby is fine, but I'm sure the mother is a nervous wreck by the time I leave. I have to remind myself babies can have all of these characteristics and still be fine.

Those of us who've had loved ones die in accidents suddenly become aware of all the sirens that go screaming through our town. Most people go right on working and may not even hear them. I have tried to ignore them, but I haven't been successful. Now I just stop and whisper a prayer for the people who have been hurt, and then I am usually able to go about my business. However, if I am wait-ing for someone and I hear sirens, I have trouble controlling my emotions.

One evening Matt was out on a date and due home within a few minutes. Glen and I were watching the eve-ning news when we heard loud sirens droning on for several minutes. We tried to concentrate on the news, but inside we both were very restless.

Finally Glen jumped up and said, "I'll be back in a few minutes."

"Where are you going," I asked.

"I have to follow those ambulances and make sure it isn't Matt."

Fear of a tragedy happening again is very real and very normal for those of us who have experienced repeated los-ses. If we allow these fears to control us, though, we will not be able to move on through the grief process.

Face Your Fears

"Forgetting the past and looking forward to what lies ahead . . . " is what Philippians 3:13 (TLB) says. Does that mean we are to forget about our children or other loved ones who have died? I don't think so, but I do feel we must release the negative aspects of their deaths so that we are free to remember them as they were before. We must release anything in the past that would inhibit our living positively in the present.

First, we must face our fears, whatever they may be:

- Another child is going to die.
- I'm afraid to let my child drive a car.
- I can't let him out of my sight because he may never come home.

- God won't let anyone close to me live — perhaps my spouse is next.

The list could go on and on depending on our individual experiences, but the effect is the same. If we submit to our fears, they will control us. *We must learn to control them.*

Find someone with whom you feel free to share your most intimate thoughts and fears. Talk them out. Sometimes, as we hear ourselves speak the fears out loud, we realize they don't make sense and we are able to release them. Unfortunately some of our fears do make sense, but we still have to let go of them.

The Bible states: "For God hath not given us the spirit of fear; but of power, and of love, and of a sound mind" (2 Timothy 1:7).

As a Christian I have learned to stop and identify what is causing my emotional turmoil. If it is fear, I then pray out loud, "Spirit of fear, in the name of the Lord Jesus, I bind you and cast you out." I have an attitude of fear which I need to get rid of.

We can often free our fears by identifying them and admitting them. As far back as I can remember, I have had a fear of water, and a fear of being too close to the edge when I am on a high place. Recently I was reminded of an event in my childhood that helped me understand these long-time fears.

When I was three years old I went with my family to Mammoth Cave. We all climbed into a small boat to tour the cave. The guide stated that the depth of the water in the cave was really not known, and she held a kerosene lantern as she talked. When she moved the lantern, it accidentally brushed against my leg and caused a very painful burn. While we were still in the boat she attempted to treat the burn. I do not remember the pain from the burn nearly as much as I remember the tremendous fear I felt that I would fall over the edge of the small boat and into that deep, deep water. It is quite likely my fears of edges and water came from that experience. Once I was able to identify the source of my fear, I could face it and start to work through it.

Just because I know I fear water and high places does not mean I should avoid fearful situations. Instead, I am able to prepare myself somewhat by talking through the situations before I get there. I know I will do better if I have a friend with me who understands my fears. I also know it is better if I admit how I feel. Then my friends can provide support.

Many parents dread the day when another child will get his driver's license because one or more of their children was killed in a car accident. My friend explained to her daughter, "The only way I can agree to your driving a car is for you to promise to respect all curfews and call me immediately if there is any change in plans. If you don't adhere to these requests, your driving privileges will be taken away. I fear another child is going to die in a car crash."

Siblings may also fear something bad is going to happen to them, and they will most surely sense the added concerns and the smothering that may come from their parents. When I was twelve, my cousin was hit by a car while riding a bike. After that, all of the other parents in the family, except mine, refused to let their children ride bikes. My parents refused to be bound by their fears and took the approach that they should just be very conscientious as they taught me bicycle safety.

My children are grown up; they have homes of their own, and live many miles away from me. After they visit us, though, I always call to see that they've arrived safely back home. If they're going to be late arriving, they stop and call us. We have all faced our fears and acknowledged the fact that tragedies can happen again. Therefore, we do everything we can to relieve our own fears and lessen the stress on the other members in our family.

When Nathan died, many of his friends' parents realized the same thing could happen in their families. One time I was visiting in a friend's home. When her son started out the door, she quickly called to him, "Wait. I didn't give you your hug!" She then explained, "Since Nate died we've realized that when a family member leaves our home it is possible he will never come back. So we always give each other a hug and make sure things are at peace between us." This family has faced their fears and then taken steps to free themselves in a healthy way.

Let your song of fear change to a song of freedom as you face your fears, understand them, talk about them, work through them, and allow yourself to be released to move through your December.

A Song of Power

Making the pain, anger and guilt
work for you

When we lose a member of our family, we think nothing could hurt us more. When our losses are repeated, though, we quickly realize that this concept is simply not true. We discover we still hurt even more deeply than we did when our first loss occurred. The pain, anger and guilt are multiplied with each loss.

The Pain

After multiple losses we wonder how much pain we can take. Some of us know we can bear more pain than we thought we could because we're still here, and we're still functioning. Glen said after Nathan died, "It's like being squeezed through a knothole for the third time. You know the pain, and you have to face it again."

Each loved one who dies represents the death of a dream. Whether it's a child in mid-pregnancy, a child who's stillborn, a child who's seventeen, or a child who's fifty, a spouse who's thirty or a spouse who's seventy, a parent— young or old—it's the death of a dream. Multiple pain will come when we have to face death one more time. One more hope, one more plan, one more dream—destroyed.

49

Making Pain Count

We can profit from our pain. I don't think anyone would want to look back on his life and say, "All of these people have died, all of these tragedies have happened, and I have not learned anything from them. I have not improved myself as far as my sensitivity to others, my love for my remaining family members, or the quality of life that I am living." The one thing I determined when Nathan died was that his death must not be wasted. We each can have that determination. We can in that way profit from our pain.

As we profit from our pain, our sensitivity to others will increase. As we progress in our grief work, we can step outside our own pain to reach out to others. Doc Blakely, the keynote speaker at the 1987 national convention of The Compassionate Friends, stated that prior to his son's death he didn't know how to help others who were bereaved, so he tended to stay away from hurting people. Now he goes to those who hurt because he knows how important it is to reach out to others in pain.

One morning Glen walked into the den and found me sobbing as I sat watching a tape of myself on a television program. He said, "Honey, what's the matter? Don't you think you did alright?"

I shook my head and said, "I did fine—but as I watched myself, I looked at that person on the screen and realized that lady's been through the fire. It's made a difference in her life."

We need to recognize that when even one person dies we have been through the fire. Use that experience. Don't let it die out, but let your experience continue to work for you. When you face your deceased loved ones someday, as I believe I will face mine, I hope you can say, "This has been the toughest thing I've ever gone through, but I made it count. Your lives were not wasted, I let God walk me through the fire and help me work through the pain. Then

I was able to share my healing with others."

I encourage you to profit from that pain.

> But now thus saith the LORD that created thee, O
> Jacob, and he that formed thee, O Israel, Fear not: for I
> have redeemed thee, I have called thee by thy name; thou
> art mine. When thou passeth through the waters, I will
> be with thee; and through the rivers, they shall not over-
> flow thee: when thou walkest through the fire, thou shalt
> not be burned; neither shall the flame kindle upon thee
> (Isaiah 43:1,2).

Reestablishing "Normal"

When someone dies, you will have to establish a new
"normal," and that means letting go of the old one. You
may try to find the old normal, but it's not there anymore.
With each person who dies, we try to find normal once
again, but the old normal is gone. Some of us keep living in
the past and aren't willing to establish a new normal. Move
on to the new normal.

One area where many people have difficulty moving on
is in doing something different with the deceased person's
room. Some families make a memorial out of the room and
refuse to touch any of the person's clothes or personal
items. Changes don't need to be made immediately, but if
after six months to a year you still are unable to deal with
that room, I personally feel you should ask a friend or a
counselor to help you confront the memories contained
within those walls. The longer you wait, the harder it will
be.

I was able to go into Nate's room immediately, and for
some reason the bedspread I bought him just months before
really bothered me. I took it off the bed the morning after
his death and asked my mother to go shopping for a new
one. Within the next few weeks I let some of Nate's friends
come in and select a piece of Nate's clothing they would like
to have. I let the rest of his things remain in the room for
about six months and then I asked my daughter to help me

sort them out. We gave some things away and I packed away those special articles of clothing that I will always keep.

It has been several years now since Nathan died, and I would say it has just been during the last year that Glen and I have found a new normal we're comfortable with. It is not the normal we would have deliberately chosen for ourselves had circumstances been different. Certainly we would much rather have our five children with us instead of just two, but we don't. So instead, we have established a pattern we can live with and we're enjoying it to the fullest extent we can. We have moved on.

It's important that you get to the point where you can let it hurt, but walk through the worst of the pain and not dwell in it. Determine to do whatever you need to do to move on: Keep a journal; talk; get counseling. Keep going until you feel that you have learned from your loss, and that you have developed an ability to reach out to others.

Your Reservoir of Love

I remember feeling after my two children died as if there were two gaping holes in my heart — I needed to give my love to them but they weren't there to receive it. Everyone who has experienced a loss has love that is waiting to be given. We need to tap that love. It's so important we don't just bottle it up and never use it. I decided there must be other kids in this world who needed love — and I was going to find them. While my kids were in high school, I found young people in their school who needed love and I poured it out on them.

As I recall the many students who crowded around to sign my yearbook, the former students who still come by to see me, and the now young adults who bring their children to see "Grandma Heavilin," I realize that in many ways I am a rich lady. I couldn't have become rich if I had stayed at home and said, "God isn't fair; I don't like what has happened, and I'm going to stay here and be mad." It would have been easy to do that. I can say, though, that through all the twenty-four years since Jimmy's death, as I have reached out to others and taken the initiative to love, God has honored my efforts. This year my oldest son's high school class had their tenth-year reunion. The reunion committee asked Glen and me to be host and hostess for that event. They decided to have someone at the door whom most of the students would recognize, and, because we had been so involved with their class, they chose us.

You have a great reservoir of unclaimed love, and you are the only one who can determine how you're going to use it. As you relinquish your song of pain to God and let that love flow out, He will bring you the comfort you need.

Dealing With Anger and Guilt

Often when someone dies, family members feel they should have been able to prevent the death. We are supposed to be able to take care of those we love. Three times in my life I have not been able to protect a child of mine from death — that makes me feel helpless. In those situations we will often feel anger and guilt.

When we see people who seem to have gone tripping through life unscathed (they have five or six children who have experienced nothing worse than a broken arm), or we look at parents who complain about the children they have (and we want to lecture them on how to appreciate their loved ones), there will be moments when we deeply resent what those families have. Then we feel guilty because of our feelings.

We may feel guilty because we talk more about the person who died than we do about the others. We think, *Oh dear, why do I talk about that one so much? They all mean a lot to me.* With my situation, I had Jimmy seven weeks, Ethan ten days, and Nathan seventeen years. Obviously, it is logical that I am going to talk about Nate more. It does not mean I loved him any more, just that I had a longer time to love him.

There may also be times when we feel angry at our loved ones for dying and that can cause us extreme guilt. *Being angry with the deceased is a natural response.* I think it's very important that you acknowledge angry feelings. Go sit at the grave and verbalize your thoughts if you need to. I experienced some anger toward Nathan, and I thought, *This is ridiculous. It obviously wasn't Nathan's fault. He had no way to protect himself from that drinking driver.* Yet when I verbalized my thoughts one day, through my tears, I found myself saying, "Nathan, why did you leave us so soon?" Even now, as I drive down the freeway and look at the Del Rosa exit, I think, *Nate, why didn't you take the Waterman Exit instead of this one?* If you have these feelings, don't be ashamed of them. Just realize it is important to talk through them with a friend or a counselor.

Using Your Anger and Guilt

It is possible to harness the guilt and anger and use them *for* you instead of letting them work *against* you. Take that energy you've been expending in the guilt and anger and turn it into power to work for you. I once heard Dr. Robert Schuler state on a TV program that when we have a problem with guilt or anger, we need to "face it, trace it, and erase it."

In my book *A Woman of Honor* I talk about how I learned to face and trace the pains of my past and erase the negative hold they had on me. I had to "hand all of these pains to the Lord and say, in the presence of a prayer counselor, 'Lord, please help me forgive those who have hurt me, forgive me for the wrong feelings I've had, and heal me.' "[1]

Once we understand the origin of the guilt and anger, we can make it work for us. As I resolved my pain from the past, I was able to gain knowledge that could help others. I have gained an understanding and sensitivity that I did not previously have. I also have been able to turn my anger into constructive power and positive influence, donating many hours each year to organizations such as MADD (Mothers Against Drunk Driving) and SADD (Students Against Drunk Driving) which were formed by others who were angry at the devastation caused on our highways by people who drink and drive.

Let God transform your dirge of pain, anger and guilt into an influential song of power as you let go of the bondage of the past and move on to a future with purpose.

6

A Song of Hope

---

*Dealing with multiple loss, violent crimes
and legal complications*

While our internal fears, pain, anger and guilt can delay
our healing, external circumstances also can be a definite
hindrance in the process.

Multiple Loss

As our traumas multiply, often it seems our friends disappear. At a time when we need extra support we become
increasingly alone. When this happens, we experience the
stigma and isolation of suffering. There are several reasons
for this phenomenon.

As our trials increase, our friends' ability to explain
away our troubles decreases. When tragedy strikes the first
time, it's easy — "Everybody has some trouble in his life."

After the second tragedy, our friends weakly mutter,
"God must really want to use you in a very special way."

By the third trauma, many friends tend to shake their
heads in dismay and go home to pray for our souls.

A woman named Kelly called in when I was a guest on
a radio talk show. She related that in the past year she had
lost her mother and a son as well as several other relatives,

and she was recently divorced. She shared that she felt so alone and that God didn't want her to be close to anyone. I asked, "Kelly, are you involved in a church?"

At that point Kelly began to sob. "Oh, yes. I'm a Christian and I have a church, but they don't want to hear about people who've died. They love to hear about the people who've been healed and about the people whose prayers have been answered in spectacular ways, but they don't want to hear from me because my relatives didn't get healed; they died. I'm all alone in my grief."

I remember feeling that people were pulling away from me when our two infants died. I'm sure some of those people were convinced the Heavilins were not living right or they would not be having so much trouble in their lives. Even I began to wonder about us this past year when it looked like our granddaughter Kate might die. I wondered if we had some kind of plague that we were now passing on to our children's children. My frustration was increased when just two days after our little Kate was born, an acquaintance asked me, "Have you ever considered having someone pray over you to have your blood lines cleansed and prevent this from happening again?" Her comment piled heaps of guilt on my already drooping shoulders.

The multiple loss family may also feel a stigma from others who have experienced a singular loss. Perhaps they fear our repeated experiences will minimize their own loss. I know that right after each of my children died, I didn't want to hear about anyone else's pain, especially if it seemed worse than mine. The multiple loss families are also a reminder to the single loss families that it *can* happen again. Often they can't face the possibility of bearing such tremendous pain again, so it's easier to avoid us.

Violent Crime

Some families have not felt the stigma of multiple loss, but they have experienced the devastation that results when the loss is due to a violent crime. Violent crimes are so public that the family often is forced to retreat. Retreating, however, isolates the family not only from the public, but also from the friends who normally would come to their aid. These families have many questions to ponder.

Here are some examples:

After my six-year-old son was kidnapped and murdered, I wondered how could God let this happen to me — when I hear so much about child abuse, abortion, abandoned children — why was I being punished?

Three months later our son's murder seemed to be a forbidden subject. Like it all happened and now I was to put it behind me and go on. I have, but it takes time. I really needed to talk to friends.

The fact I lost a six-year-old is very hard to accept. At first I felt I couldn't laugh or enjoy myself. I felt guilty for having a good time.

When my adult son was murdered, it didn't help for people to tell me that it was "God's will." I felt that my son was a victim of our social system that allows so many criminals to roam the streets with guns. The Civil Rights Act has allowed many criminals to know that they might never have to pay the penalty for their crimes. Although two of these people are serving life terms, the murderer has been tried and sentenced to the gas chamber, but has never been executed.

I do not think my son's murder was "God's will." He was a victim of the times we live in. There are so many evil and wicked people in this world and I don't believe that God would say, "Now you go kill this good young man." It is still very hard for me to understand why it had to happen.

Legal Complications

Whatever the cause, and whether premeditated or accidental, a person's death which is caused by someone else nearly always involves subsequent legal activities, and they create additional pain for the family. After Nathan's death, I discovered that additional pain. I felt completely out of control. I was unable to prevent my son's death; I could not control the insurance company; I couldn't control the district attorney. I couldn't even control my own calendar. My schedule was subject to sudden change because of attorneys and judges whom I didn't even know!

Others have experienced this same frustration. I met Jim at a book-signing party for *Roses in December*. As he walked toward the book table it seemed every muscle in his body displayed anger. I could sense his anger as he dropped a book down on the table. His conversation was very terse and when I asked what grief he had experienced, he blurted out, "My son was killed by a drunk driver!" My thoughts jumped back to the emotional pain we experienced as we worked through all of the legal complications following Nathan's death, and I understood Jim's anger.

After I signed Jim's book, Glen took him aside to invite him to attend a meeting of The Compassionate Friends. That was almost a year ago. Jim has since become a good friend of ours, and I am grateful that he is willing to share his story.

An airline pilot, Jim was in New York City when he received a call informing him that his sons Mark and Miles had been in an accident and both were in serious condition. He made some calls himself, and finally he was informed that Miles had died.

Jim recalls:

As I was waiting to get a flight from New York back to California, in spite of my numbness, I managed to make about twenty phone calls. I will always be grateful for the kindness of the man at the hotel who wouldn't let me pay for the calls, and I remember that the taxicab driver wouldn't take a tip when he heard why I was flying back home.

When I got on the plane, I said to the pilot who was a personal friend, "Miles is dead. My baby is dead!" After the plane was in the air, the hostess came back and talked with me, held my hand, and let me cry.

When I got off the plane, my family was waiting for me and it seemed everything must be all right. I remember saying to them, "Miles is all right, isn't he?" And once again I heard those words, "Miles is dead."

It was only then that Jim found out his son's death had been caused by a drinking driver. The story Jim told me after that is very typical. No one in the drinking driver's car was seriously injured, but Jim's son was dead and his other son was severely injured. His children were the innocent victims.

To Jim and his family, it was an open and shut case. After drinking too much the man had gotten into a four-wheel drive vehicle and then proceeded to drive down a mountainous road at high speed. The driver tried to pass on an extremely blind curve at that speed and lost control of his vehicle, hitting Miles' pickup head-on. Jim felt sure the man would be convicted of felony drunk driving and vehicular manslaughter.

After many months of postponements of both pre-trial hearings and of the trial itself, finally the man agreed to plead guilty to felony manslaughter with gross negligence. The maximum sentence was six years in prison, but after many legal maneuvers, the man was sentenced to eight months on a work release program based on assumed good behavior.

Even though the driver is presently on probation, Jim has received reports that the man has continued to drink and drive—one more frustration for the bereaved family. Most victims I have talked with state they have felt added pain when there appeared to be little repentance on the perpetrator's part.

I asked Jim what this has done to his family and he told me, "Most members of the family have sought professional help; even two years later we are still experiencing a great deal of grief. My remaining son has felt so helpless since he was never even asked to be a witness at the trial—he was denied the opportunity to represent his dead brother. My daughter has changed her profession and is now training to be a counselor, and our confidence in the legal system has been completely destroyed."

Unfortunately Jim's story is not unique. Whether a person has been killed by a drinking driver, murdered, or killed in some other deliberate manner, or whether the death was caused by someone's gross negligence, I have seldom met a family who feels the case has been resolved satisfactorily. I realize that no amount of punishment or financial settlement will ever bring a person back or heal broken hearts, but today it seems that most legal proceedings not only do not cause healing, but they also create deeper wounds.

As Jim and I talked, we agreed that nothing that the victims or their families do can guarantee a satisfactory outcome to a legal action. There are some efforts they can make, however, which will help them know they did everything possible, and friends of the victims can encourage them in their endeavors.

Establish a rapport with the district attorney

After our son was killed by a drinking driver, in my naiveté I assumed the district attorney would be contacting us, would want information from us, and would keep us informed on the manslaughter case. I was wrong. I have since discovered the prosecuting attorney seldom contacts the victim's family unless they were witnesses to the crime, and even then it may be a long time before they are contacted. The only way we ever received information about the case was by calling and calling, and finally writing the prosecuting attorney a very strong and emotional letter. He then gave us an appointment and explained the legal procedures we would be facing.

We did discover that most district attorney's offices have a victim's advocate office that will talk with the families and at least let them know the legal procedures and when trial dates have been set. That office also will provide information on how victims who are in need can obtain financial help.

Another rude awakening victims' families will have is that in a criminal case the defendant has the right to hire any defense attorney of his choice that he can afford. The victim and his family have no choice as to which deputy district attorney will represent them. Actually the prosecuting attorney represents the state and often it seems the victim has no one to represent him. Also while the defense attorney may have as much as six months to prepare his defense, often, as in our case, the deputy district attorney may have had as little as a few hours to prepare his case because his case load is so immense.

By pursuing the opportunity to meet and talk with the deputy district attorney in charge of our case, Glen and I were able to let him evaluate us, too. Apparently he was able to assess that we were intelligent, generally rational people who were willing to help him represent the state and our son in the best way possible. After that first meeting, he saw to it that we were kept informed on all of the legal proceedings.

Solicit support agencies

Today there are many organizations available to help victims of violent crimes. Some of those organizations give psychological and emotional support; others will offer legal advice; some will provide both areas of expertise. Start with your local district attorney's office and find out if they have a victim's advocate program. That office may be able to recommend other agencies to you. Sometimes these groups are listed with the Chamber of Commerce or you can find them through the reference desk of the city library.

Distribute petitions

In certain cases, such as when laws should be changed

or when elected officials need to be reminded of the concerns of their constituents, petitions can be a powerful tool.

Solicit letters of support

Letters of support for a specific position can have influence if they are sent to the local newspapers, the deputy
district attorney and his superiors, or the presiding judge.

Do your homework

Before you solicit people to help you with petitions,
writing letters or filling the courtroom, it is very important
that you become knowledgeable about the facts of your particular case and the details of the laws which would apply
to your case. Your attitude should never be threatening or
accusatory. People who are out of control when they confront officials of influence will be dismissed as "one more
emotional, out-of-control, angry person," and will seldom
get a favorable reaction from the powers that be.

Even though criminal charges are not made, frequently victims of a wrongful death still can decide to enter into
a civil suit against the perpetrator. Malpractice suits and
cases where a death occurred because someone made an
error in judgment or because machinery malfunctioned
would fall into this category. These cases are generally even
more lengthy than criminal actions, though, and often do
not come to trial for four to six years. I have talked with
some families who have won the civil suit and received fairly large sums of money and others who have sat through
weeks or months of court proceedings only to have the case
dismissed, a mistrial declared, or have the jury decide the
defendant bears no financial responsibility to the victims.
Unfortunately, regardless of the outcome in the courtroom,
I have not met anyone who was satisfied with the results.
Even when large sums of money are awarded, of course it
does not bring the loved one back, and the legal process
keeps the emotional wounds open for a very long time.

I would not make a blanket statement that no one

should ever enter into a wrongful death suit, but I would caution you not to be surprised at the frustrations you will experience — regardless of the legal outcome.

Glen and I chose not to enter into a civil suit, but we did still receive a financial settlement from the insurance company. I remember the day we received the check which read, "In payment for the wrongful death of Nathan James Heavilin." How can you put a price on a family member? No amount of money will ever remove the ache in my heart. I wanted to tear up that check!

Sometimes, however, we are able to do something for someone else because of a settlement in a wrongful death case. Jim is in the middle of a civil suit right now, and he has a dream of what he will do if he ever receives a settlement. Jim hopes to buy a condominium in a quiet resort setting where other bereaved families could go for a quiet retreat, and where information and grief support could be provided for these hurting people.

Multiple loss families and victims of violent crimes need friends around them who will walk through their sorrow with them. In most cases, much of the healing process is delayed until the legal matters are resolved. The friends who are there to offer hope and encouragement along the way are invaluable. It always helped me when my friends attended the legal proceedings with me, and I appreciated their letting me talk out my feelings and frustrations. With friends — and God — to help us, we can turn our songs of despair and desolation into songs of hope and healing.

A Song of Forgiveness

7

*Overcoming the devastation of losing
someone from AIDS or suicide*

After a death, there often is a need for forgiveness. In the event of a violent crime, the family has to deal with the perpetrator. Please understand that forgiveness does not mean we are releasing a person from his responsibility in a crime or that we won't press charges or expect restitution. Forgiveness removes feelings of vengeance, resolves anger that may consume us, allows us to leave the problem in the district attorney's hands, and permits us to proceed in our healing process.

Forgiveness of ourselves must come when we have inadvertently caused a death. Several times this year I have listened to the stories of heartbroken people who accidentally caused the death of a friend or family member. Their pain is cruelly intense and they continue to bear enormous guilt feelings. It is important that these people receive strong support from other family members and from their friends. Whether there was actual negligence or the guilt is imagined, it is vital that this person have some professional counseling. He probably will have to talk out the events repeatedly with his family and any others involved in the tragedy. As he gets help and is able to voice his feelings of guilt and remorse without fear of condemnation, forgiveness of himself and healing of his pain eventually will come.

Another need for forgiveness arises when a person feels that shame, reproach, and other negative reactions have been brought to himself and his family by the death of a family member from AIDS or suicide.

AIDS

Each person in the family will experience his own individual response to the disease and to the patient when someone in his family is diagnosed as having AIDS. Often the family doesn't know a person is homosexual until he tells them he is an AIDS patient. Sometimes admitted homosexuals have been alienated from the family, but when they discover they have AIDS, they return home hoping to restore their relationship and find someone to care for them during their final days.

These circumstances increase the normal stress that a family experiences when someone is dying. Added to that is the fact that when a family member dies of AIDS, the family usually feels ostracized from those who normally would support them in bereavement, and the needs of the family often go unmet.

During the dying process and after the death, the family members probably will experience many emotions such as anger, blame and guilt, all directed toward the one who contracted AIDS as a result of his lifestyle. When someone contracts AIDS through a needed blood transfusion or through an accidental entry of the virus into the body, the family's anger may be directed toward a doctor, a hospital, or even the homosexual community.

These families all will need special understanding and patience from those around them. For proper emotional healing, they eventually will need to come to a point where they can forgive every person they see as involved in the problems and stigma that have been brought into the family. This includes, when necessary, the homosexual himself.

Regardless of how a person has contracted AIDS, he and his family need acceptance and support from those close to them.

What is the responsibility of the Christian community in these cases? I have one Christian friend who is a nurse and has volunteered to care for patients with AIDS in the hospital where she works. When an elder from her church found out she works with AIDS patients, he commented, "Don't ever shake hands with me again!" How the Lord's heart must have ached when He heard that man's response.

An approach to AIDS that would seem both sensible and Christian would include:

Be knowledgeable

AIDS is a frightening disease. We know so little about it, and with the disease comes automatic isolation and hysteria. No one has all the answers, but now there are a growing number of organizations where we can gather quite accurate information. I recently sat through a four-hour seminar on "AIDS and the Family" sponsored by the Department of Social Relations at the University of Loma Linda and presented by Dr. Harvey A. Elder, chief of infectious diseases at the Jerry L. Pettis Memorial Veterans Hospital and professor of medicine at Loma Linda University School of Medicine.

Dr. Elder stated AIDS is *not* transmitted by:

1. Close family contacts (same room, sharing kitchen, dishes, glasses, bathroom, toilet, tub, telephone, etc.)

2. Food and laundry (even when patient fixes food or drink, washes dishes or does laundry, shares silverware or glasses)

3. Body care (bathing patient, sharing tooth brush, razor, etc.)

4. Affection (hugging, touching, kissing on cheek or on lips)

5. Swimming pools

Dr. Elder stated that AIDS *is* transmitted by:

1. Sexual transmission

2. Needles and syringes

3. Paranatal (If the mother is infected, the baby's blood at birth will contain HIV [AIDS] antibodies from the mother.)

Dr. Elder concluded that "the AIDS virus enters the blood stream via an opening in the skin or a needle puncture, and rarely, if ever, does the virus cross intact mucosal membranes."[1]

Be caring

I am not suggesting we should ignore the fact that a family we are trying to help is dealing with a communicable disease, but for us as Christians, the family's needs should take precedence over our fears that we might "catch" AIDS. Jesus Christ set an example for us as He willingly interacted with lepers, prostitutes, and other social outcasts of His time.

The family who is caring for a patient with AIDS will need some physical help. It would be wonderful if churches were willing to adopt such a family. They could provide relief and rest for the family by offering to care for the patient while the family gets some much needed rest, runs errands, or just gets away from the situation for a while. They could assist with patient care by bathing or feeding him, doing his laundry, or cleaning his room. They could relieve the family by spending time with the patient, reading and talking with him, taking him for a walk or a ride, or just listening to him share his thoughts, fears, and dreams.

We also can support the family members by listening

when they want to talk about their suffering, anger, disappointment, fear, and possible feelings of guilt or blame. We can cry with the family, and after the patient dies, we can encourage the family to tell stories and share pictures and mementoes of their loved one. We can find out what support groups in our community would be available to the AIDS patient and his family, and we can help put the family in touch with those agencies.

After the patient with AIDS has died, we should be sure to remember the family on the loved one's birthday, anniversaries, and holidays. Let them know how important that person was. Don't ever give them the feeling that because their loved one died of AIDS, he did not count.

Make a special effort to bring the family into your home and be seen in public with them. Sit with them in church and make certain they are included in activities.

Often when a homosexual child comes home with AIDS, he brings his lover with him or wants the lover to be allowed to visit him. Parents who have fought their child's lifestyle and have resented and perhaps even blamed the lover, are going to feel immense anger. Make room for their anger; let them talk it out. Don't defend or argue — just listen. I have to be honest. If I were faced with that situation, I'm not sure how I would handle it, but I do know it would be very difficult for me to live in peace after my child died if he had died still alienated from the family. I feel it is important that we help families to somehow make peace with a dying child because in the long run it will help the child die in peace and the family to live with themselves in peace after the child's death.

Suicide

It is common, when someone dies, for the survivors to ask why. Why did he have to die so young? Why did she suffer so much? But when someone takes his own life the survivors are plagued even more with these unanswered questions and with feelings of anger and frustration toward the deceased person. Since I have not experienced this type of loss, I sent out questionnaires to some families I knew who had. I am grateful to them for their willingness to answer my questions so openly.

Though technically not an accurate term, the remaining members of the family of a suicide victim are referred to as "survivors of suicide." In the following section I am simply stating some of the issues that these survivors of suicide wrestle with, along with some answers to the questions I asked them. I also am including some statements that appeared on the surveys, with little further comment from me.

As I read through the surveys, I became aware that one question appeared on almost every questionnaire: "If God is a sovereign God and controls everything, why did He let this happen?"

One parent wrote:

> God is sovereign, so it's very hard to picture Him watching her taking her own life. Of course he gave us all free will . . . yet in her depressed state, she was irrational, and she needed protection *from herself*. On the bulletin board above her desk, she had copied these words from Psalm 32:8: "I will instruct you and teach you in the way you should go; I will counsel you and watch over you" [NIV]. I don't know how long that had been up there, but oh, how it hit me after she was gone! The words *watch over you* spoke of *physical* protection to me then, and I wondered what it all meant. He could have stopped her . . . even if she *is* better off in heaven with her Savior, what of the 'non-testimony' it would be to all our neighbors, her high school and college friends, those she had witnessed to of the value of having Christ in one's life to meet *all one's needs?* Would they turn even further away from Him, since He didn't meet her need in her darkest hour? It's all very confusing. I guess I *have* to believe that "God is related to my loss" in that He can work good out of it, and already has.

Survivors of suicide often experience a greater sense of helplessness, anger, and guilt than those who have lost a loved one in an accident or through an illness.

My anger has been pervasive and overwhelming at times. I suspect that I displace my anger because I have become enraged with myself and everyone I know, but never with my son. My anger is deeply entwined with guilt because when I begin to feel any anger with him, I stop and feel guilty. I also feel guilty about being angry at all. In addition to this, all of my angry feelings with my parents and ex-husband, which were deeply buried, have resurfaced and I have to resolve them now—a sort of Pandora's box has been opened. Someone has told me that when I get over being angry with myself, I will then be able to be angry with my son. I don't know. Sometimes I think this rage is truly a form of cancer, eating away at me, slowly killing me.

At first I was overwhelmed with the "why's" and the "what I might have done's." I shall never know why he chose this option. I believe I was the best mother I knew how to be. Certainly, in retrospect, there are things I would have done differently, but at the time I did the best I could. A suicide is the ultimate rejection. He's gone forever—and by choice.

I cannot express in words the feeling of such absolute futility and frustration of having struggled to raise a child as a single parent without any support, thinking you have done a fairly good job, only to have your Life's Project impulsively and willfully destroy himself on the threshold of adulthood.

The aim of this book and particularly this section is to help us understand the ways we can help the bereaved and to recognize the hindrances to healing. I asked my friends to share particular acts and words that helped them or that didn't help them work through their grief.

What did help?

My friends and co-workers always allowed me to talk and really hung in there with me. I felt they cared. Friends called a lot to lend their support. We've even had deep discussions about death at work. I appreciate it when people ask why my son killed himself because it means they are interested and allows me to unload some guilt through explanations.

Two of my co-workers shared with me the fact that there had been suicides in their families. It helped me to know that someone I worked with was understanding. Another co-worker had lost her father to a heart attack the previous October. She was very sympathetic and understanding. She talked with me a great deal about my son's death and the fact that he committed suicide. We talked of possible reasons for his death, what he was like, what his life had been like and we talked about him being in heaven. Many times she initiated conversations about him. We also talked a great deal about her father and the circumstances of his death. We understood each other's feelings and helped each other through some extremely difficult days.

My oldest sister has always been my best friend. She has been supportive of me since my son's death. She has listened patiently, she's talked with me, cried with me and grieved with me. She doesn't tell me how to grieve and she understands that it will go on forever. She knows that she can't feel the depth of my loss and she doesn't try to minimize it. She and another sister have gotten books for me to help me deal with my grief.

The mystery and extreme pain of our kind of tragedy is something I would have said I could never have survived. It had to be all the prayer and the grace of God that kept me from falling apart. The ones who let us talk about her and the tragic way she died, and those who listened and asked questions really helped. As her mother, I needed to talk about her devotion to us and the Lord. Letters from folks who had experienced or were close to a similar death were a great help, because of the stigma of our kind of tragedy.

One family member who has very conservative views of his faith wrote to say that he knew that God had forgiven my son and we who are left can do no other than to forgive him also. He also said that God had given him to us for twenty years and we should be grateful for that and remember the good parts of those years.

It helps me tremendously to be able to help others. I have a great need to try to save others from such an experience and have focused my volunteer work on young people (especially boys) who mostly need to talk to someone and find out that there's always hope.

What didn't help?

I have detected pity in some people, and I resent this.

I returned to work a few days after my son's suicide. My presence at work was not acknowledged by half of my co-workers. My family won't talk about my son. Perhaps it is too hard for them or they are afraid of hurting me by talking about him. It hurts more when they don't talk about him.

After my father's suicide, our pastor shared with our congregation that my father had died in a tragic accident, which couldn't have been further from the truth. Consequently, when I returned to church I was pretty much alone with my grief. Not one person in our Sunday school class asked how I was doing or expressed their sympathy. This went on for several weeks and my husband and I were really feeling hurt and angry. Finally, about one month after my father's death, I got up during praise time and shared with the congregation about my father's death and I requested their prayers as I was having a very difficult time. Because of my taking that "reaching out" step, I am now receiving the support I need from my church family. Suicide is such a devastating way to lose a loved one. I didn't know where to turn at first. I couldn't reach out to God as there was so much anger. If you ever lose a loved one through suicide, be honest. Don't "hide" the truth. That's the worst thing to do!

I also asked these families to share what consequences of their loss were the hardest to accept and here's what they listed:

- The fact that I have no more children.
- I'll never be a grandmother.
- Guilt that I contributed to his suicide.
- This may have been preventable and it may have been an accidental suicide.

Another response was:

> When we sold the house we lived in at the time of my
> son's death, we had to include a statement about a suicide
> having taken place in the house. It hurt me to have to do
> that. It made it seem that there was something wrong
> with us and our home. The people who purchased the
> house had had a suicide in their family. They were very
> sympathetic and understanding.

The "Unpardonable" Sin?

A woman who called me when I was a guest on a radio
talk show expressed a fear that often eats away at the
suicide survivors. Lillian's granddaughter had committed
suicide just a year earlier when she was twenty-three. Lillian sobbed as she said, "My Christian friends have told me
that I will never see my granddaughter again because since
she committed suicide, she will not go to heaven."

My first reaction was rage. How could anyone possibly
think it was necessary to say that to Lillian now that her
granddaughter was dead? What purpose would it serve?

I asked, "Lillian, was your granddaughter a Christian?"

"Oh, yes, I led her to Christ myself. I know she was a
Christian."

I answered, "From what I read in Scripture, the basis
upon which we will be admitted into heaven is whether we
have received Christ as our personal Savior, not on how we
died. If your granddaughter received Jesus Christ as her
personal Savior, I believe you will see her again when you
arrive in heaven." As we continued talking, I could hear the
relief in Lillian's voice.

Since that time, I have studied Scripture very closely to
make sure I gave Lillian the right answer. There are five
completed suicides mentioned in the Bible: Samson, Saul,
Ahitophel, Zimri, and Judas Iscariot. The Bible teaches
that Samson and Saul were leaders appointed by the Lord,

and they belonged to God. I have not been able to find any Scriptures to indicate that their position with God changed after their suicides. They were still His children.

Suicide is the murder of self. The Bible teaches that we should not kill another human being. Yet we see examples in the Bible of people being forgiven of murder. David, Moses, and Paul are some who come to mind. In the event of suicide, the person usually would not have had time to ask God's forgiveness of that particular sin before he died, but that could be true of other types of deaths as well. If God could forgive murder of others, how could He not forgive self-murder?

First, I believe no one could possibly understand suicide more than God himself because He has the ability to know what goes on in a person's mind that would make him think suicide is the best thing for him. Surely God's compassion and forgiveness are there for a Christian whose mind has become confused and depressed. Second, I'm sure many of us will come to our Father with some sin still unconfessed, but we are still God's children if we have invited Him into our lives.

> My sheep hear my voice, and I know them, and they follow me: And I give unto them eternal life; and they shall never perish, neither shall any man pluck them out of my hand. My Father, which gave them me, is greater than all; and no man is able to pluck them out of my Father's hand (John 10:27-29).

I hesitated to write this section for fear someone would misunderstand and quote me as saying it is not wrong to commit suicide. I have not said that. Suicide is sin. It is as wrong as murder, rape, or any other violent crime, and those who commit suicide will have to face the Lord Jesus Christ with their sin just as the rest of us will have to with ours. However, I have found nothing in Scripture that depicts suicide as the "unpardonable" sin.

I am not writing this as a theologian, but simply as a

woman who sees the hearts which are broken because a family member committed suicide or died of AIDS. These families need our constant support and understanding as we patiently lead them to a point where they can forgive others — and themselves — and tenderly sing the song of forgiveness.

THE HELPERS

*Share each other's
troubles and problems,
and so obey our Lord's command*
(Galatians 6:2, TLB).

8

A Song of Assurance

---

*How friends and professional caregivers
can assure the family*

When we got to the hospital after Nathan's accident, it was the typical emergency room scene. We were asking many questions and we couldn't get any answers. No one would tell us anything. The hospital staff handed us some insurance forms and asked us to fill them out. We could hardly think what our name was let alone names of insurance companies and automobile license plate numbers. We kept asking, "What about our son?"

Finally they took Glen in to talk with a policeman. He told Glen nothing about Nathan; he just confirmed the fact that our car was involved in the accident. We later realized that Nathan was probably two cubicles away from Glen, but Glen never got to see him.

We watched a nurse come and talk to the other family in the emergency room. We assumed someone in this family was involved in the accident. The nurse told them their family member was injured severely, had received a blood transfusion, would most likely survive, and would be going into surgery immediately. In a few minutes, when they brought a person on a stretcher through the hall, I recognized the light brown hair and size eleven feet—it was

Nathan. But then my question was, "Do you know who you have? Maybe you've gotten them mixed up." I almost lost control at that point. I think I nearly leaped over the nurses' station in my attempt to talk with someone. I had a panicky feeling that they didn't even know who they had. The nurses just kept assuring me that someone would talk with us soon.

Finally, a nurse came out and acknowledged that it was in fact our son they had taken to surgery. The other injured man was still in the emergency room. She told us about the extent of Nathan's injuries. Because of my previous experiences of having buried two sons, I just looked at her and said, "Do you think he's going to make it?"

Her eyes lowered and she shook her head, "No."

It was important for me to have the truth at that moment. I needed to know how to pray; I needed to know what to say to people as I called them. Shortly after that, the nurse came back to tell us that Nathan had died. Glen and I hugged each other. We felt like the life was draining out of us. Our little family had spent most of the evening alone, asking questions, trying to gather information, but there was no one at the hospital to help us.

Since there was no family room available, the nurse asked us to go into the nurses' station while we waited for the surgeon to come to talk with us. She informed us that the surgery was never begun because they could not keep Nate's heart going long enough even to start it. When the surgeon came down from the operating room, my first thought was, *For being a noted surgeon, this man seems to be awfully nervous.* His hands were visibly shaking. We spent our time comforting him and telling him everything would be OK because we knew Nathan was in heaven. We later discovered the man who talked with us was a resident and not the attending surgeon. The only contact we've ever had with the surgeon was when we received a bill from him for $1500, even though he never performed surgery or any other services for Nate, except to be on call.

As we left the emergency room, the nurse handed me a brown grocery bag with Nathan's Nike basketball shoes in it. His shoes seemed almost sacred to me just then — certainly much too important to be placed in an ordinary brown paper bag. I felt so helpless and empty.

Warm Memories/Cold Feelings

As many of you read this, I'm sure you're thinking, *She thinks she had it bad; she ought to hear my story.* I have heard, and have read many of your stories. This letter, which appeared in an Ann Landers column, is an example of our all-too-common experiences:

> *Dear Ann Landers: Please educate your readers today. I am talking about the way deaths are handled in some institutions.*
>
> *When my parents and I went to the hospital to be with my husband, we were told he had gone into cardiac arrest and had been taken to the intensive care unit. A nurse ushered us into a small room to "wait."*
>
> *The room had two chairs, a table and a phone. There was no clock, no tissues and no water to drink. We were kept in that room for two hours with no word from anyone.*
>
> *Finally, when I couldn't stand it any longer, I went to the nurse's station to find out what was going on. "Oh," the nurse said, "hasn't anyone asked you who your mortician is?" That is how I got the news that my husband had died.*
>
> *After the funeral the hospital bills arrived. I paid them the following week. Thirty days later I received a bill listing my husband as an "outpatient." I was charged for treatment and medication given a week after his death.*[1]

I feel certain Nate received excellent medical care, yet, like the lady in the article above, our experience at the hospital was not a positive one. However, I can honestly say I have no negative feelings toward that particular hospital. I believe the hospital personnel did everything they knew how to do for us, and I am confident they did everything they could for my son.

Since I have dealt with the deaths of three children, I can compare how I felt after each experience. Jimmy died at home. We were able to hold him as long as we wanted to before the coroner came. Even though it was a negative experience for us, the memory is still warm. Ethan died in a hospital, after twenty-four hours of being near death. The nurses often came to sit with us in the private room that had been provided. They talked with us and cried with us. The doctors came in frequently to give us a play-by-play of what was going on. I saw the doctors weep, too. We were able to hug each other and recognize there was nothing we could do in this situation except comfort each other. Although I wish it had not been against hospital policy to allow us to be near Ethan and touch or hold him, I have warm memories about the experience. It is not hard for me to drive by or even to enter that hospital.

The medical center which cared for Nathan is special to me because that is where my son died, but I have cold feelings when I think of our experience that evening. No one reached out to us. It doesn't have to be that way. I believe it can be different. There can be warm feelings even about a negative situation.

Acknowledging the Family

In our recent experience with our little granddaughter Katherine, I saw firsthand that a hospital can do their job efficiently and still not shut the family out.

When we arrived, the doctors were furiously working over Kate, but they purposely left the ICU door open and encouraged us to stand at the doorway and watch as they cared for *our* baby. The doctors came to the door frequently to give us an update and even allowed us to step a little closer to take pictures of Kate.

After the transport team from Children's Hospital arrived, the ICU door was closed, but as each staff member entered or exited, they held the door open for a moment and said, "Take a peek."

While the transport team continued to prepare Kate for her twenty-five mile trip to the Children's Hospital, the attending physician invited all of us into our daughter-in-law Debbie's room. He spoke very candidly about Kate's chances and all of the complication possibilities, yet he was very gentle and patiently answered all of our questions.

After Kate had been settled into the portable isolette, she was wheeled down to Debbie's room. The family was invited to come in. The transport team doctor opened the lid of the isolette and helped Debbie touch little Kate who was now about four hours old. The floor nurse came in with a Polaroid camera and took several shots of Matt and Debbie next to the isolette. The staff spoke positively, but we were quite aware we might be saying hello and goodbye to Kate all at the same time. They gave us as much time as we needed.

When we arrived at Children's Hospital, we were told that parents and grandparents had twenty-four hour visiting privileges, and the doctor made sure we would give Debbie the telephone number. He stated, "If Kate's mother wakes up at 2 A.M. and wants to know how Kate is doing, you tell her to call the hospital and we will let her talk to Kate's private nurse."

When I went in to visit Kate for the first time, she was about eight hours old. The NICU [Neo-natal Intensive Care Unit] nurse showed me how to touch her and stroke her, and she encouraged me to talk to her. Glen and I visited her several times that evening, and Matt spent most of the night by her little crib.

How grateful I am to the personnel at each hospital for continuing to assure us that Kate belonged to our family, and we did not have to relinquish our rights as family members just because she was in the hospital. I am confident that our involvement, our constant presence, talking, and stroking, had a lot to do with Kate's miraculous recovery.

We also appreciated the sensitivity the hospital personnel displayed to Debbie. She was in a semi-private room, but the other bed was empty. The nurse told her they would try very hard not to put anyone else in her room so that she could have privacy and would not have to watch another mother attending to a new baby. Debbie told me that when a friend's newborn baby had to be taken to another hospital, each new shift of staff asked the mother where her baby was. Unfortunately, this also happens occasionally when a newborn dies. If the mother is still assigned a room on the maternity floor, she also may have to endure the pain of watching other mothers feed and care for their babies while her empty arms ache.

I know of one hospital that makes every effort to place the mother in a room separate from the maternity wing after the death of a baby. They fasten a pink or blue teardrop on the mother's door to warn hospital personnel that a baby has died and this mother is grieving.

Medical Personnel

Whether the family is experiencing a sudden trauma or the effects of a patient's long-term illness, someone needs to be available to acknowledge their pain and answer their questions.

The evening Nathan died, as we sat alone in the emergency room, we were plagued with many questions such as:

What are they doing right now?
Is he conscious?
Is he in pain?
What will they do in surgery?
Will he live?
Why is it taking so long?

Are they sure it's our son?

If a caregiver had been there to help us find the answers, our attitudes and feelings about our experience at the hospital would have been quite different.

Through our activities as members of The Compassionate Friends, Glen and I are aware of several families who have been involved in malpractice suits. I know that medical personnel pay attention when they hear the word *malpractice* because most of them fear legal battles. I have observed also that many of these cases started out with the families saying, "I don't understand why they did what they did"; or, "I asked the doctor some specific questions and he never gave me answers I could understand. I felt he was avoiding me."

When those caring for our loved ones don't answer our questions, we are left to create answers of our own – and quite often our answers are wrong. Most of us aren't well-versed in medical technology and procedures, so it becomes important that medical personnel take time to answer our questions thoroughly. Many of the malpractice suits I am acquainted with would have been stopped or never started at all if there had been better rapport between doctor and family, not just between doctor and patient.

Those who are medical personnel, clergy, funeral directors and in law enforcement are generally among the first people to confront the deceased's family. Whether the family is experiencing a sudden trauma or the culmination of a long-term illness, their pain needs to be acknowledged.

The night Nate died we definitely felt that nobody wanted to acknowledge us, and they really wished we weren't there. Hospitals need to have someone, especially in the emergency room, who can be assigned as a caregiver. Sometimes chaplains can serve in this capacity. In our particular situation, no one even asked if we wanted a chaplain.

The caregiver needs to be someone who is comfortable with trauma situations. He doesn't necessarily need to be a medical person, just someone who will not be afraid of death—someone who can talk to people and serve as a liaison between the family and the doctors and staff. The caregiver can help with such questions as: What's happening to our loved one right now? Can you call a chaplain for us? The caregiver could mediate between the family and the doctor, helping to build rapport among those involved. He could help the family make phone calls. Fortunately, the night of Nate's accident our son Matt remembered to grab a roll of coins before he left the house. There was no phone available except the one public pay phone—of the three installed—that was not out of order that evening.

It's important that the hospital provide privacy for the family. I realize this provision depends on budgets and priorities of that particular hospital, but the family needs a place where they can talk and grieve privately. It was quite uncomfortable for us, and I'm sure for the family of the drunk driver who had hit Nate's car, because we spent the evening sitting across from each other. They saw the nurse tell us Nathan was dead, and they knew his death was caused by their family member.

Handling With Care

I would encourage professional caregivers not to be afraid of the bereaved, but do be gentle with us. This is one of the most intimate and difficult times a family will ever go through. Touch us, hold our hands, and cry with us. Families need the help and encouragement of everyone they come in contact with, especially during those first few hours.

Our Ethan died more than twenty-two years ago, but I still remember the name of the nurse who tended him, and I could describe her to you because she cried with us and hugged us. She shared her own sorrow with us, and she acknowledged us.

Obviously doctors and nurses cannot allow themselves to get emotionally involved with each of their patients or they themselves would soon suffer burnout. However, it is possible to be sensitive to hurting families simply by acknowledging them and then treating them with dignity and sensitivity.

A study at UCLA revealed that, in ordinary circumstances, just to maintain emotional and physical health, men and women need eight to ten meaningful touches a day.[2] Imagine how many more touches and hugs we need when a loved one is dying.

A nurse who heard me speak once called me later and said, "I decided to take you up on what you said about touching people." An older man had come in with his wife who had had a stroke. When the nurse went to get the husband to have him talk with the doctor, she called him by his first name and said, "The doctor would like to see you now." Then she put her hand on his shoulder as she walked with him to where the doctor was waiting.

She told me, "I noticed everyone else did exactly as you had described. They skirted him and stayed away from him because they didn't want to face the issues of his wife's condition."

Three days later, after the wife died, the man came back to the emergency room to find this nurse. He said, "I want to thank you for everything you did for me."

The nurse was amazed. "All I did was call him by name and touch him as we walked to the doctor's office." To her, those efforts seemed so little and unimportant, but the man remembered.

I read in the *UCLA Journal* of a neurosurgeon who decided to see if it made any difference whether he touched or didn't touch people when they were his patients. For a week, with half of his patients, he stood by their bed, talked with them, spent a certain amount of time with them, asked how they were doing and showed great concern. With the other half of his patients, he sat on their bed or touched them on the knee or put his hand on their shoulder, but otherwise did exactly what he had done with all of the others. At the end of that week he had the nurses survey all of his patients, asking them to estimate how much time the doctor spent with them that week. Those patients whom the doctor had touched estimated that the doctor had spent twice as much time with them as did the people he hadn't touched.[3] Now he serves all of them in the same way as far as meeting their medical needs, but his interest and concern are shown by letting himself be just a little bit more vulnerable with some of his patients. He reaches out and touches, and it makes a difference.

A compassionate caregiver can help the bereaved stop singing December's song of confusion and loneliness and begin to sing a song of assurance by taking time to answer their questions, consider them in decisions, and reach out to them in a sensitive manner.

A Song of Consideration

Answering the family's questions

I sent a survey to about forty different families I have met over the past few years who have experienced the loss of a family member. I asked them to score their treatment by medical personnel, clergy, morticians, law enforcement agents and lawyers. Along with medical personnel, the clergy got the lowest marks. Many of the families felt the clergy were unwilling to spend time with them and unable to answer their questions. Most commented that they seldom saw the clergy again after the funeral.

A bereaved father wrote:

> *Our minister did the best he could, but he didn't provide the comfort I believe a minister should be capable of giving. I needed a spiritual perspective that he couldn't provide. That added to the anger. Pastors should get adequate training in dealing with newly bereaved parents. They should provide or make available resources for the bereaved to learn to adjust mentally, physically, socially, and spiritually.*

A member of the family of a suicide victim wrote:

> *I would think that in this very difficult and painfully mysterious type of loss of a deeply committed Christian child, the pastors would have felt we needed regular spiritual counseling to keep us from falling apart or be-*

coming bitter against God. Suicide is a heavy, heavy event with which to cope. Our church is large, with many pastors, and I would have thought this kind of a death warranted repeated pastoral calls and visits without our request for them. Perhaps they themselves felt inadequate to deal with this type of death with all its horror.

The Pastor's Role

One friend related that about a month after his son's death, the pastor did call and ask, "How are you doing?"

Ben thought, *Finally someone is interested in us,* so he took the risk of answering honestly and said, "Well, pastor, we're really not doing very well. My wife and I are having trouble talking to each other, and I'm depressed most of the time."

There was silence. Finally Ben realized that the pastor couldn't handle his openness, so he pulled the mask of peace back over his heart and said, "Oh, really pastor, I'm just having a bad day. All in all, we're doing just fine."

The pastor muttered, "Well, I'm glad to hear that," and quickly ended the call.

Why would a pastor do something like that? First, because he has not been prepared to deal with the bereaved. Few seminaries deal with the subject of death except to teach future pastors how to conduct a funeral. Second, often when we are open with him and try to describe the hurt inside of us, he thinks we expect him to have a quick fix. Since he doesn't have a way to patch us up and take the pain away, he feels uncomfortable around us and finds it easier to stay away. When we say we're doing "just fine," he feels better and doesn't feel obligated to meet our needs.

Few of the bereaved are looking for a quick fix. It doesn't take us long to realize that our problem can't be taken care of quickly and we don't really expect anyone to fix it. What we do need is knowledgeable people around us who will listen and at least discuss our questions with us.

Pastors should be well versed on what their particular denomination teaches on the subjects of heaven, hell and salvation. What is heaven like? Is my loved one there? What happens to babies when they die? If my loved one committed suicide or a terrible crime before he died, can he still go to heaven? Will we know each other in heaven? What part did God play in all of this?

Most bereaved people will appreciate a pastor who has thought through these issues and has come to some conclusions and is willing to interact with his parishioners on these topics.

I have spent a lot of time thinking about the sovereignty of God in the past few years. I have searched the Scriptures and formed what I hope are biblically based opinions on the subject. However, when I have wanted to bounce my ideas off of someone else, I have had difficulty finding clergy who were willing to interact with me. I am very grateful to one pastor friend who has been willing to listen to me and read my writings to make sure I'm still on track. He hasn't judged me when my theories have seemed strange or out in left field; he has just patiently guided me toward what the Bible says.

When a loved one dies, even the unchurched and most non-religious people will start thinking about heaven and a life after death. It behooves pastors and churched people to be ready with some well-documented answers.

Funeral Arrangements

Although most of us will have had some prior relationships with doctors, hospitals and clergy, few of us know much about mortuaries and cemeteries. We probably will choose both on the basis of a friend's or clergyman's recommendation, with little knowledge of the type of questions we should ask.

Through our experiences, I have discovered the importance of planning before there is a need. I have asked my parents to write down their preferences as to funeral and burial arrangements. I heard of one pastor who asked each member of his church to fill out a form to provide instructions for their funeral — songs to be sung, verses to be read, pallbearers, people to be notified, burial instructions. He is a very wise and practical pastor.

Those of us who have planned funerals or dealt with mortuary and cemetery personnel before can be of great help to the newly bereaved. So often after a funeral I hear people say, "I wish we had thought of that."

After her son Brent was killed by a hit and run driver, Linda called me and asked if I would help the family plan the funeral. A relative of Brent's had attended Nathan's funeral and was impressed with how it was conducted. I spent the afternoon with Linda and just had her tell me about her son. Brent was a vital, active, enthusiastic young man with a contagious smile. We decided it would be good to have a collage of pictures of Brent at the funeral for friends to see.

As I was leaving, Linda said, "I wish I could tell other parents how much we should value the time we have with our children." I suggested she write something up and include it in the program, and she did: "Take time for your children and express daily your love for them — for we know not what tomorrow brings."

The funeral program also included a blank sheet of paper on which we were to write something special that we remembered about Brent. Linda was then able to put all of those notes in a scrapbook that she could read for years to come.

What I did for Linda was very simple, but it added a special dimension to Brent's memorial service that will help the family know they honored their son in an individual and unique way.

Mortuaries could provide a similar service to their clients by compiling a notebook that would show examples of programs and ideas from other funerals. Most bereaved people feel they have lost all of their creativity and are very appreciative of helpful suggestions. We had a program printed up for Nathan's memorial service, but I would not have thought to do that if I had not seen it done at a previous funeral.

I wish we had taken time to choose a cemetery plot before we had the need. There are too many decisions to be made too quickly. Cemetery personnel need to be patient with the family, and they should show the family all of the alternatives available in making the decisions.

Generally, families feel a need to rush into ordering the gravestone also. One mother wrote:

> *We ordered the words: "Precious Daughter" on our daughter's tombstone and later regretted that we hadn't said "and sister" for the sake of all her sisters. We just didn't think of it. Also we only had the years of her birth and death, and we wished we'd included months and days as well. Perhaps the funeral or cemetery director could have gently suggested these two additions, without pressure, just in case we forgot — which we did.*

Our two infant sons are buried in Michigan where I was raised and where my parents lived until 1984. My parents moved to California and now there is no one in Michigan to visit our boys' graves. We considered moving the caskets to California, but we quickly realized that it would be very costly and not a wise use of our money. However, Glen and I still feel a need to be able to acknowledge our sons — here in California. Just this year it dawned on me that I could have two more flower containers installed at Nathan's grave. Once I thought of it, I ordered them immediately. I felt so much better when I went to the grave this Christmas and was able to place flowers in *three* vases and acknowledge all three of my dead sons.

While I was talking with the sales personnel at the cemetery, I discovered that it is possible to have Jimmy and Ethan's names carved on Nathan's gravestone if I include "Also in memory of" by their names. Oh, I wish I had known that earlier. Cemetery personnel should inform families of all such options. Even though it means we will have to have the marker completely redone, I believe Glen and I will do that in the near future. I have since thought how simple it would be for cemeteries to have a "Memory Garden" where families could have flower containers installed with simple little markers naming people they would like to remember but who are buried in other parts of the country.

There are a number of details connected with funeral arrangements which will need to be taken care of, and I have put together a checklist which I hope will be helpful. Many of these things can be done by a close friend or family member.

__ Call the pastor

__ Call relatives

__ Call family attorney

__ Locate any existing will

__ Call insurance companies

__ Locate all insurance policies and bank accounts

__ Check on existing retirement funds

__ Notify Social Security

__ Help write obituary

__ Help plan funeral

__ Go with bereaved to mortuary and cemetery

__ Provide guest book to use at bereaved's home

__ Find someone to provide family meals

__ Clean the house

__ Mow the lawn

__ Grocery shop (especially for munchies and finger

foods, paper products: tissues, toilet tissue, towels, plates, cups, napkins, etc.)

___ Do minor house and car repairs

___ Have someone stay at house during funeral

___ Have someone record food and flowers brought to the home

Whether the caregivers are clergy, medical staff, morticians, police, lawyers, or friends who want to help, as they answer our questions and show consideration to us and our grief, the song of consideration will create an environment in which we can move much more successfully through our grief work.

A Song of Consolation

---

*Meeting family needs when someone dies at
the hospital, or has chosen to die at home*

The 1986 volume of the *Journal of Consulting and
Clinical Psychologists* presented the results of a survey of
families who had gone through grief. These families were
asked to state what things were helpful and what were unhelpful.

Unhelpful Responses

Listed as unhelpful were advice giving, minimizing the
situation or trying to force cheerfulness, and inappropriate
identification with feelings.[1]

Advice giving

Often in the first few hours bereaved families are not
ready to hear how they should handle their situation and
their grief. They don't appreciate being told, "You will get
over this"; or, "Things will be better in a few weeks or
months"; or, "You'll have more children and forget all
about this."

Minimizing the situation or trying to force cheerfulness

The families also stated they didn't appreciate it when
people minimized the situation or tried to force cheerfulness: "He isn't in pain any more." "At least you had him

for seventeen years." "Oh, well, be glad you have other children."

Also, when those of us who have experienced grief talk to the newly bereaved, we need to be careful that we don't just point out all of our victories and fail to acknowledge the time, effort and pain it took to arrive at a point where we could function in a somewhat normal fashion again.

Inappropriate identification with feelings

The article continued to note the families did not appreciate an inappropriate identification with feelings: "I understand how you feel." Unless you have buried three sons, it is impossible for you to know how I feel. Even if you have buried three sons, you may not know how I feel. Relationships are different; situations are different. There may have been something going on between me and one of those children that would make his death even more difficult. It is all right to say, "I've lost a child, and I know how I felt." Perhaps you could share some of your feelings, but don't suppose the other person is experiencing identical feelings to yours. Each situation contains its own unique qualities.

Helpful Responses

This same group listed several things that were helpful: contact with a similar other, expressions of concern, opportunity to ventilate feelings, presence of another person, and complimenting the deceased.

Contact with a similar other

Listed as most helpful was contact with a similar other. Hospital personnel, clergymen and morticians can be key in connecting a family with others who have gone through a similar situation. I would suggest that they compile and provide a brochure including the names, addresses and telephone numbers of organizations in their area which could be helpful to families in trauma. People who are grieving seldom have the energy to find these resources on their own. It took Glen and me over a year to find the numbers and contact our local MADD and The Compassionate Friends chapters.

A grieving family should never leave a hospital empty-handed. All I can remember is walking out of the hospital carrying that dumb old grocery bag with Nathan's Nikes in it. As I share with numerous hospitals, quite often I hear a gasp as I talk about the grocery bag because they realize they have done that same thing. There are better ways to handle the situation. A plastic bag with a zipper closing at the top and an insignia of the hospital on the side would be acceptable. Or the belongings could be wrapped and sealed. Those belongings seem almost sacred to a bereaved family and they will be acutely aware of how the belongings are handled.

Rather than just walking out with a bag of belongings, the family should have something placed in their hands that will give them hope of being able to survive this ordeal. It would be helpful for hospitals to make a little folder of items which could include a pamphlet of comforting Scriptures, a booklet appropriate to the specific type of loss, a bereavement card signed by the chaplain, and a resource list which should include phone numbers of support groups in the area and recommended books on grief. The family needs assurance that there is someone they can call and someone who will be willing to listen to them in the days and months to come.

Expressions of concern

It's all right for professionals to say how bad they feel, and it's all right for them to extend their sympathy. Their vulnerability will bind them to the bereaved family, and it really makes a difference in how the family will respond to them. As I look back on the situation with Ethan, with what I know now, I wonder why Ethan wasn't taken to a larger hospital, perhaps a children's hospital. If he had been, it is possible his life could have been saved. Yet, I have never felt angry about it, because those doctors stood with me, cried with me, hugged me, and I know that they did everything they knew to do. I know the nurses poured their lives into our baby that evening. They shared themselves with me and let me see their vulnerability, too, and I am grateful to them.

Opportunity to ventilate feelings

Professional caregivers should remain calm when a bereaved person yells and screams. If it were their loved one dying, they might feel like yelling and screaming a bit, too. It's OK. It won't hurt anybody, and it may get some of the person's feelings out so he or she can talk with the caregivers in a reasonable way.

Presence of another person

This is different from a similar other. It includes anyone who can be with the family. This is where the caregiver can say, "I'm here, and I'm going to help you and stick with you through this event."

Complimenting the deceased

There may be times when doctors and other caregivers have worked with this person before and have had opportunity to watch him deal with his illness. With my little Ethan, even though he was only ten days old, the doctor made the comment, "He was a real fighter." That made me feel I could be proud of my child, and it showed that the doctor cared, too, because he was observing something personal about Ethan. Our baby wasn't just one more patient.

Law enforcement people sometimes can give us details about our loved one's last moments that will provide comfort.

This interesting statement was made at the end of a report in the *Psychological Journal:* "Instead of teaching support providers about specific strategies, it may be more important to teach them how to manage and control the anxiety inherent in their interactions with the victim."[2]

In other words, if doctors, nurses, clergy, or other caregivers have some death experiences that have not been resolved in their own lives, or if they've had some professional/client relationships that have not been resolved, they need to work on those and deal with them.

When a professional caregiver becomes as whole a person as he can be, he won't have to be afraid of me when he has to tell me my son is dying. Professional caregivers tend to do as the rest of us do—they carry unresolved things from their childhood, and from their adult lives, into trying situations, and then the client or the family becomes the innocent recipient of those frustrations.

Donating Organs

I am sorry no one talked with us about the possibility of donating some of Nate's organs. I would love to know that someone else was helped even though Nathan died. After I spoke to one group of emergency room personnel at a large city hospital, one of the doctors told me, "I have had many occasions where organs could have been used and I had patients who needed them, but I was afraid to broach the subject with the patient's family. I just have trouble talking to them about such things."

I suggested he contact a donor organization and take some training from them. Those organizations will usually send someone out to talk with the family if there is time, but I am sure they would also be happy to train doctors and other medical personnel in the proper ways to approach a family.

Closure

The family also needs a chance to say goodbye to the

deceased. Somehow that evening, no one in our family was ever asked to identify Nathan or was able to touch him. It really could have been someone else because he was never legally identified. Glen and I both wish we had seen him. We wish we had had a chance to just have a prayer of committal and to say goodbye. We didn't have that opportunity.

MADD research has shown that

> . . . surviving victims are able to proceed in their grief processes better if they have been able to view and touch the body than if they have not. Although it is intensely painful, it gives one time to feel some closure with the victim and to enable one to move out of denial about the death. Victims who have not been able to see or touch the deceased often report a nagging belief that the victim may still be alive. They may expect the victim to call or walk in and convince them that it was all a joke. While the memory of the deceased viewed in the emergency room or morgue may remain a source of nightmares and painful memory, it is generally a better choice for the surviving victims than avoidance of the body.[3]

In an article entitled "Funerals Are for the Living," Lois Duncan tells that because her family never had open caskets, she continued the tradition when her mother died.

> I never saw my mother's corpse—and I never allowed anyone else to. When well-meaning friends began arriving at the funeral home to "view the remains," I was horrified. I insisted the casket be kept closed, the way I knew Mother would have wanted it. I was never totally convinced she was in it.
> Today—over fifteen years later—I still am not convinced. I have frequent dreams of receiving a telegram announcing that Mother has "finally been located" and that the report of a fatal heart attack was incorrect. I awake from those dreams confused. Then, as reality takes over, I am overwhelmed by a rush of pain as raw and all-consuming as it was on the day she died.[4]

The writer goes on to explain that she was quite upset when her husband's family insisted that their mother's casket remain open, but on the day of the funeral she made an observation:

> I went over to the casket and looked down at my
> mother-in-law. To my surprise, I felt in control of my
> emotions. I had grown used to the figure in the box – and
> to the fact that it was only a shell that once had encased
> a person I loved. I felt a bond with others who had
> gathered to say goodbye.
>
> My husband and I returned home and fell back easi-
> ly into the normal pattern of our lives. I will not pretend
> that we didn't feel the loss . . . I did not, however,
> awake shrieking her name in the night. And although my
> husband dreamed about his mother often, the dreams
> were not painful.[5]

Glen and I both admitted later that we really could not
accept in our minds that Nathan was dead until we walked
into the funeral home and saw him in the casket. The last
time I saw that boy he was bouncing a basketball and walking out of the school. The next time I saw him, he was in a
casket. It would have helped if we had had the transition
of seeing him at the hospital to realize there was no life
there.

When a child is stillborn or dies as a newborn, most
hospitals now take pictures. I agree with that practice in
any situation where it is possible to do so. Someone in the
family can be told the pictures are on file if they ever want
to see them. Two and a half years after Nate's death, I realized I needed to see the pictures from the accident. When
I requested them from the district attorney, he gulped and
said, "That's a little unorthodox."

I said, "That's OK, but I have to see the pictures."

I can't say it was easy to look at them. It wasn't. I took
them home and then carried them around the house and
cried and cried, but it was healing for me. I also discovered
that Nathan looked a whole lot better than I had thought
he would look. I had built up in my imagination a picture
of what he would look like, and actually, Nathan looked the
best of anyone in the accident, although the others lived

and he died.

I think that, even if the person is terribly disfigured, someone in the family needs to see the deceased. If the closest family members don't think they can handle it, that's all right. Choose someone more distant, maybe a chaplain, who could tell them later what the person looked like.

Caregiving

Being a caregiver is not an easy job. Often you will have to give people news they do not want to hear. They may even lash out at you and you may have to take anger you don't deserve. In the midst of all the turmoil, try to remember what a strategic part you play in the healing of hurting people.

William R. Dubin, M.D., has written:

> The psychological needs of survivors of sudden death may be overlooked because of the pressure of time and the urgent needs of other emergency patients. Empathic intervention with families who have suffered such a loss is very important. A failure to recognize the dynamics of grief and attempts at premature closure of grieving can have serious consequences for the survivors. A staff that is aware of the needs of the grieving person and can facilitate this process will help cushion the trauma of loss and set the basis for a healthy grief process.[6]

Choosing to Die at Home

The situations I have mentioned most often in this book refer to someone who dies suddenly and unexpectedly. However, death does not always come quickly, even for children or young adults.

I first met Dana at a seminar, and she told me that her sixteen-year-old son Jon had been battling osteogenic sarcoma for more than two years. After a partial right leg amputation and aggressive chemotherapy, the doctors felt Jon's chances for survival were quite good.

Dana had faced the possibility of Jon's death, and then she saw him improve, but she still experienced many of the stages of grief even though Jon had not died. As we talked, Dana admitted that one of the most frustrating factors was that the family had no guarantee they wouldn't be thrown back into the agony of grief, because they knew Jon's remission could end at any time.

Within a few weeks of our meeting, Dana called to tell me the doctors had found more cancer. The remainder of Jon's right leg and hip were amputated and he would have to go through even more horrendous chemotherapy — for another year.

Dana recalls:

> *Jon had been complaining about his left shoulder at that time but the doctors did not believe there was anything other than pain from an old injury, or possibly Jon, being too worried about the spread of cancer, might be imagining this. So, to pacify Jon, they X rayed the shoulder. It was devastating when cancer was discovered there also. Jon said, "Doctor, am I going to die?" and the doctor said, "Not if I can help it, Jon." Jon asked for more details. The doctor said Jon had a 10 percent chance of survival, that he would begin chemotherapy immediately, and surgery on Jon's arm would be performed in a few months if the cancer did not show up anywhere else.*
>
> *In a few months, Jon was told the cancer had spread to his lungs. Chemotherapy was stopped, and Jon was told he had six to nine months to live. The next morning, after that visit with the doctor, I found this note on my refrigerator:*
>
> > *My dearest Mother, I really do love you very much so let's spend the rest of the time we have together in peace, love, harmony and laughter.*
> > > *Love, Your Son,*
> > > *Jon Philip Fladhammer*
>
> *Peace, love, harmony and laughter — good advice for all of us!*

In one of the early chapters in this book I described the

four basic temperaments: Sanguine = fun; Choleric = control; Melancholy = perfection; and Phlegmatic = peace. I explained that all of us will react to grief differently depending upon our individual temperaments. Based on those temperaments, we also will react in different ways to the prospect of dying.

Dana writes:

Because Jon and I were of like personalities I understood how Jon could joke around and have fun, how he could enjoy the attention and going and doing things at full speed ahead. Unfortunately, some other people with opposite personalities had a difficult time understanding this. It is too bad that we often try to force our own expectations on others. A few weeks prior to Jon's death, his doctor had a talk with him about the fact that it wasn't normal for him to be so "up" all the time and that he needed professional help because he was not "dealing with" the situation. It was at this point, coincidentally or not, that Jon became housebound. This conversation did "take the starch out" of Jon temporarily. Not only did the doctor not really understand Jon (especially his Sanguine personality), but, did he really understand the power of the Holy Spirit in Jon's life? Jon's personality was only one witness to the phenomenal strength and power of our Lord Jesus Christ.

During the last few weeks of Jon's life the family never really discussed home versus hospital; they just all knew they wanted to be at home. Dana commented: "One advantage of being at home is that it is HOME (as Webster says, a congenial environment, on familiar ground). Even under these critical circumstances, it was still relaxed and comfortable."

Not all families would choose the route Jon's family chose, but medical personnel should always give families the opportunity to make this choice if it is at all feasible. Most areas have home health service organizations which can provide medical equipment and a visiting nurse, give instructions to family members, and deliver prescriptions at the request of the family doctor.

When someone is ill at home, we can utilize many modern day conveniences that might normally be called luxuries. Jon's family installed a private telephone line and cable TV for him, used the VCR frequently to watch Jon's favorite movies, and put their answering machine to good use. Dana says:

> *I have a whole new respect for the answering machine and would sooner have given up my refrigerator, I think. When Jon was hospitalized I kept people informed of details with the message on the machine. After Jon was housebound, we could switch it on if necessary, without worrying about missing the call.*

When someone chooses to die at home, the family needs much support. Friends could offer to sit with the patient while family members sleep or tend to necessary errands. Friends can buy groceries and bring in prepared food. I would caution you always to call the family when you wish to visit. Often the home will have to be run on a schedule very similar to that of a hospital, and at certain times visits would be very disruptive. However, most families will always welcome a telephone caller who genuinely wants to know, "What can I do for you?"

I am most appreciative to Dana for being willing to share her thoughts with me. At the time she wrote to me, Jon had only been gone four months. I feel I would be remiss if I did not emphasize that Dana knows this whole ordeal would have been almost impossible to bear if it had not been for the power of prayer. She concludes:

> *Overall, we had very little difficulty caring for Jon those last few weeks when he was housebound. It was the greatest privilege and source of joy I have had. I am so thankful it was not necessary to share this with hospital staff. God does give you the strength when you need it, as you need it. And, the heavens were continually bombarded with prayers.*
> *You see, Jon had asked how he would die. And he was*

told he would probably choke to death or gasp for air. But that Sunday morning during the church service people were praying that Jon would die peacefully in his sleep. God answered those prayers as he has answered so many prayers. Jon just went to sleep in the arms of Jesus. This was truly a miracle.

Only later did I realize, the last conscious thing Jon did was reach up and touch my face — the last and most precious of many beautiful memories.

Whether we are lay or professional caregivers, as we sing the tender song of consolation we will help people survive their Decembers and rebuild their lives so that they can sing a new song.

THE HEALER

He is despised
and rejected of men;
a man of sorrows,
and acquainted with grief . . .
Surely he hath borne our griefs,
and carried our sorrows . . .
and with his stripes
we are healed
(Isaiah 53:3-5).

A Song of Confidence

Finding peace with God in the midst of suffering

As I mentioned in an earlier chapter, I travel around the country and talk with the bereaved and I learn more and more that when someone dies, often the most non-religious people begin to think about God and even the most religious begin to ask questions about God.

I have been a Christian for more than forty-six years. I have read through the Bible many times, and I have had the privilege of sitting under the teaching of some noted Bible teachers. Yet each time one of my sons died, and when my little granddaughter's life hung by a thread, I struggled with who God is and what influence He had in the day-to-day happenings of my life. I want to share with you what I have discovered through personal Bible study, questioning of Bible scholars, and personal observation. I want you to know that it's OK to examine the reasons for the events in our lives.

When our twin sons were born on Christmas morning of 1965, just a year and a half after the death of our seven-week-old son Jimmy, we knew the twins were a special gift from the Lord. We wanted to tell the world how good God had been to us—giving us an extra son perhaps to pay us back for the one who had died. We sent out over a hundred birth announcements proclaiming Psalm 118:23: "This is the LORD's doing; it is marvellous in our eyes."

It was easy to give God the credit when everything was going our way, but when Ethan died ten days later, I felt like God had tricked me. What would my friends think now? What could I say to them? God and I had many conversations in which I told Him how I felt, but as time went on, I began to see that God was using our experience to make us stronger and wiser people. He had also given us a special compassion for others, especially young boys. As my love began to grow for boys who were not my own but needed a second mother, I thought perhaps I could begin to see God's plan.

Then Nate died and I started to ponder things all over again: *This may be the Lord's doing, but it doesn't seem very marvelous in my eyes.* Why would God allow all of these things to happen to one family? Through the years I have discovered that the concept that bad things don't happen to good people is a myth, but I have still struggled with the question, *Why* do bad things happen to good people?

The first question I had to settle in my mind was, Does God really have anything to do with what happens to His children?

Some people say, "Well, obviously He knows these things are going to happen because He is God and He knows everything, but He didn't plan them or allow them. A loving God wouldn't do that. He just watched while they happened."

Others say, "Satan is in control of this world at the present time, and God doesn't have anything to do with the bad things that happen to us. The consequences of sin are out of His control.

Then others say, "All of the bad things that happen to

us are our fault because we have made wrong choices. We bring all of our problems on ourselves. They have nothing to do with God."

I listened to all of these comments, and I did not feel at peace with any of them. I couldn't see that my children or I had made wrong choices which could have caused their deaths. What wrong choice did Nate make? He was following all of the rules of the road, he wasn't playing around, he was obedient to his parents, he honored the Lord – but he is still dead. Jimmy and Ethan were too little to make choices, good or bad.

The Bible refers to Satan as the ruler of "the darkness of this world" (Ephesians 6:12) and as "the god of this evil world" (2 Corinthians 4:4, TLB), but it also teaches that even Satan is subject to God and cannot touch one of His children without God's knowledge and permission. "And the Lord replied to Satan, 'You may do anything you like with his wealth, but don't harm him physically' " (Job 1:12,13, TLB). " 'Do with him as you please,' the Lord replied; 'only spare his life' " (Job 2:6, TLB). Although Satan is running free in this world, I always thought God had ultimate control over His children, those who had received Him as their personal Savior. Before Satan could touch God's servant Job, he asked God's permission.

I also reasoned that, since God is all-knowing and was aware that each of my children was dying, as He also is an all-powerful God, He had the capacity to change their situations if He so chose. He could have directed Nate to take a different road, kept the drunk driver off that road for a few seconds more, or simply allowed Nate to escape serious injury. I cannot conceive of serving a God who was powerful enough to rise from the dead but not powerful enough to control Satan. It seems to me that would make Satan more powerful than God, and if that's true, we're all in trouble.

As I read Scripture and reasoned through all of these

theories, I came back to my previous conclusion: God allows His children to suffer. Then I began to search for an answer to the question, *Why* would a loving God allow His children to bear so much pain and suffering?

In a little booklet entitled *The Furnace of Affliction,* Pastor John Emmans presents three reasons God allows Christians to suffer: to correct, to comfort, and to conform.[1]

To correct

> You have forgotten that word of encouragement that addresses you as sons: "My son, do not make light of the Lord's discipline, and do not lose heart when he rebukes you, because the Lord disciplines those he loves, and he punishes everyone he accepts as a son."
>
> Endure hardship as discipline; God is treating you as sons. For what son is not disciplined by his father? If you are not disciplined (and everyone undergoes discipline), then you are illegitimate children and not true sons.
>
> Moreover, we have all had human fathers who disciplined us and we respected them for it. How much more should we submit to the Father of our spirits and live! Our fathers disciplined us for a little while as they thought best; but God disciplines us for our good, that we may share in his holiness.
>
> No discipline seems pleasant at the time, but painful. Later on, however, it produces a harvest of righteousness and peace for those who have been trained by it (Hebrews 12:5-11, NIV).

When troubles come our way, we would not be wise if we didn't take time to examine ourselves and make sure there are no obvious sins in our lives. Parents help children stay on the straight and narrow by disciplining them when they stray from the right path, and the Bible teaches that God will do the same thing when His children are getting into trouble. Please understand, God's discipline is not meted out as a vengeful punishment, a "getting even." Rather, this word has more the connotation of training and instruction. God, as our heavenly Father, disciplines His children to teach them acceptable patterns of life and behavior, the same as responsible earthly parents do.

When Nate died I did some soul searching. Some people would say, "Certainly God wouldn't let your child die because you were sinning," but Scripture would not back up that theory. In fact when David sinned by getting involved with Bathsheba, the child born of that union died.

> And David said unto Nathan, I have sinned against the LORD. And Nathan said unto David, The LORD also hath put away thy sin; thou shalt not die. Howbeit, because by this deed thou hast given great occasion to the enemies of the LORD to blaspheme, the child also that is born unto thee shall surely die (2 Samuel 12:13,14).

The Bible teaches that God does use suffering to discipline his children, but it does not support the theory that *all* sickness, death, and suffering come because we are sinning.

To comfort

The Bible also teaches that God allows us to suffer so that we might be benefactors of His comfort and then be able to comfort others in His name.

> Blessed be God, even the Father of our Lord Jesus Christ, the Father of mercies, and the God of all comfort; who comforteth us in all our tribulation, that we may be able to comfort them which are in any trouble, by the comfort wherewith we ourselves are comforted of God (2 Corinthians 1:3,4).

Before Jimmy died, if friends of mine lost a child, I would have sent a card and probably attended the funeral. The first time I saw them I might have acknowledged their loss, but I doubt that I would have mentioned the death again unless they brought it up. I would never have thought to remember them on the anniversary of the death or on the child's birthday. I think I would have been quite insensitive to their pain.

When Jimmy died, as I was greeting friends at the funeral home, I noticed that those who had experienced a

loss similar to mine were much more sensitive and con-
cerned. They knew the hurt I felt and they understood how
long that pain would last. They never said, "You should be
over this by now." They knew how to comfort me.

Now, twenty-four years and two more funerals later, I
understand the special gift of comfort God gives to those
He has allowed to suffer. As I sat with a radio host on a call-
in talk show, we received many calls from grieving people.
They would ask me questions and tell me their stories—
and the host would shake his head in disbelief. Sometimes
he would look at me and helplessly shrug his shoulders as
if to say, "What can you possibly say to help this person?"

As I listened, I silently prayed, *Lord, give me the discernment to know what is really bothering this person. Let
me sense where she has become stuck in the grieving process.*

One lady whose Christian son had been involved in a
fatal accident after drinking at a party told me she didn't
feel comfortable at church any more, but she didn't know
why. As we talked she admitted she resented the people at
church because her child had died and it didn't seem
anyone else was having any trouble. Then I said, "Mary, if
I were in your situation, I think I would feel some anger
toward my son."

I could hear the sobs on the other end of the line as Mary
said, "I am so mad at him. He knew better. He knew how
we felt about drinking. He embarrassed our family. Now I
feel everyone at church is looking down on us. But then I
think, 'He's dead. How dare you feel anger toward him.'
And I go on a guilt trip and get depressed."

Later the radio host said, "How in the world did you
know to ask Mary about her anger toward her son? I would
never have thought of that."

I smiled and answered, "I've been there."

I've since communicated with Mary and she is working

through her grief in a healthy way now that she has been able to identify where she was stuck. I know God uses my successes and my failures to help me help others in their grief work.

I recently received this letter:

> *This past July I met and spoke for some time with you and your husband at the Christian Booksellers' Convention in Anaheim, California. I know you'll remember me, for we discussed our experiences with grief—the loss of your sons and for me, the loss of my husband. At that time you autographed your book for me and shared Romans 8:37: "But despite all this, overwhelming victory is ours through Christ who loved us enough to die for us" (TLB).*
>
> *Your book,* Roses in December, *was truly a blessing to me. I read it when I got back home and since then I do "keep looking for the roses." The Lord's leading in my life since that day I spoke with you has been a special rose from the hand of God, for it has been the turning point that I've been searching for since my husband's death.*
>
> *The first two and a half years of widowhood found me looking for someone the Lord might have for me. Though I was willing to leave the choice with Him, it became increasingly difficult to accept that He had chosen not to send that someone. Now because of having met you, reading your book and a number of other books, I feel the Lord leading me into a ministry for hurting people. Since that day in California, He has taught me to stop dwelling so much on the past and move on with life.*
>
> *Thank you for caring and sharing with me, for being there at the right place and right time—His time—and for all you've meant to me.*

I would never have chosen for my life to go in the direction it has, but when I read a letter like the one above, I feel grateful that I was in the right place at the right time. What a privilege to be able to comfort fellow sufferers, to encourage other weary souls and see them go on to serve the Lord and use their difficult experiences to comfort others.

To conform

I believe God has a special plan in mind when He allows

suffering to come into our lives. However, I must admit that when I was in the midst of grief, I didn't really appreciate "friends" quoting "And we know that all things work together for good to them that love God, to them who are the called according to his purpose" (Romans 8:28). I could see no good in the death of an innocent child.

Yet, as I read the verse which comes after that verse, Romans 8:28 became a little more palatable: "For whom he did foreknow, he also did predestinate to be conformed to the image of his Son, that he might be the firstborn among many brethren" (Romans 8:29).

So part of the good that is to come out of our troubles is that we *conform* to the image of Christ — we become more Christ-like. The catch is, we have a choice — to be or not to be conformed.

Some years ago I attended a seminar conducted by Bill Gothard. He compared each Christian to a diamond in the rough. The diamond's beauty will be revealed through the polishing process. Our lives are like diamonds, and how much diamond is left after the polishing process of life depends on how much we resist the bumps and bruises along the way. The diamonds cannot be polished without friction, nor man perfected without trial.

When you're in trouble, what kind of a person would you turn to for help — one who has never had any troubles and has seemed to float through life on the proverbial "cloud nine"? I don't think so. I think we tend to be drawn toward a person who has been through a polishing process, one who has become strong through adversity. I want to be one of those strong people, a diamond that has not resisted the polishing process.

We have a choice to make. We can sing a song of defiance and say, "I will never serve a God who allows such terrible things to happen," or we can choose to sing a song of confidence. We can be confident that even though we don't understand why God has allowed these events to come into our lives, "He that keepeth thee will not slumber" (Psalm 121:3).

He has a plan for each of us individually.

"The steps of a good man are ordered by the LORD: and he delighteth in his way. Though he fall, he shall not be utterly cast down; for the LORD upholdeth him with his hand" (Psalm 37:23,24).

He is worthy of our trust and will delight in hearing us sing our song of confidence in Him.

A Song of Surrender

Learning to let God have control

I agree with the three reasons we discussed in the previous chapter which Pastor Emmans gave as to why God allows suffering. It is true that God uses difficult times to discipline His children; He allows His children to learn how to comfort others by receiving comfort from God; and He uses the difficult times in our lives to conform us to His image. I agree with these three reasons, but I would like to add a few more observations.

I believe God allows troubles and trials to come into the lives of His children to reveal to us our insufficiency, His sufficiency, and His sovereignty.

To Reveal Our Insufficiency

I have never been more aware of my insufficiency, my inability to control the happenings in my own life, as when I stood near my child while his life slipped away and he died. I realized my only hope was in the Lord.

As King David pleaded for his child's life, he, too, recognized his insufficiency to change the course of events, but through his experiences he adopted the philosophy which he presents in Psalm 34:19: "The good man does not escape all troubles—he has them too. But the Lord helps him in each and every one" (TLB).

David made the choice to acknowledge his own inability to escape trouble and follow the God who gave him the ability to face and overcome his troubles.

In contrast to David's response, we read the story of Pharaoh as he continued to hold the Israelites captive in spite of all of the pestilences God brought upon him. As with David, God allowed Pharaoh's son to die because of Pharaoh's sin. David and Pharaoh were both shaken by this discipline. Pharaoh became angry and bitter and his heart became hardened toward God, but David acknowledged his insufficiency. He repented and allowed God to soften his heart. The Book of Psalms is a testimony to David's softening process as he became a "man after his [God's] own heart" (1 Samuel 13:14).

Pharaoh determined to outsmart God. Although he repented of his sins long enough to allow the Israelites to leave the land of Egypt, he soon allowed the bitterness to build again, and he pursued the children of Israel. It cost him his life.

We have the same choice today. As we find our lives out of control, we can continue to say, "I can do it myself," or we can say, "God, I can't handle this on my own. I am handing the controls over to you. I'm anxious to see what you can do with this mess."

To Reveal His Sufficiency

As we yield the reigns of our life to God, we will become aware of His sufficiency. As Job watched his property be destroyed, his children taken from him, and his health deteriorate, he still knew God was faithful as he said, "Though He slay me, yet will I trust in Him" (Job 13:15).

The psalmist David states:

> I am radiant with joy because of your mercy, for you have listened to my troubles and have seen the crisis in

my soul (Psalm 31:7, TLB).

And God responds:

> I want you to trust me in your times of trouble, so I can rescue you, and you can give me glory (Psalm 50:15, TLB).

One mother wrote:

> *God and religion were not an important part of my life prior to my son's death. However, during the depths of my depression, I found a new, more personal relationship with God. I pray often and feel He has manifested Himself to me by answering my prayers for help and by comforting me.*

Connie's six-year-old son was kidnapped and brutally murdered, but Connie stated, "Out of this tragedy has come a strong spiritual life for me. I thank God each day for being alive and for all the beautiful things in this world and for my other son whom I adore. He has brought me lots of joy and pride."

A mother whose only son died said, "His death drew us closer to God, made us more dependant on Him and a lot less materialistically minded."

After her father's suicide, Tricia wrote me:

> *So many different things have happened since my father's death; some good, some bad; but one special thing is I've grown so much in the Lord. I have learned to rely on His sufficient grace to get me through each day.*

Through much pain and suffering, these people have come to grips with their own insufficiencies and have recognized that only God is sufficient to meet our needs. Once we come to that point, we will be able to grow through our grief.

To Reveal His Sovereignty

I believe God also desires that we see and understand His sovereignty. Often when people face tragedy, they have

to reevaluate their concept of God. When good things happen to us, it is easy to say, "God did this for me." When
things happen to us that we perceive as bad, it is hard for
us to acknowledge that God could possibly have anything
to do with our troubles.

Scripture makes it very clear, though, that some of our
difficulties, infirmities and traumas come so that the Son
of God may be glorified:

> And as Jesus passed by, he saw a man which was blind
> from his birth. And his disciples asked him, saying,
> Master, who did sin, this man, or his parents, that he was
> born blind? Jesus answered, Neither hath this man
> sinned, nor his parents: but that the works of God should
> be made manifest in him (John 9:1-3).

God does not originate or orchestrate sin, but I do
believe we define some things as bad which are not. For example: For the Christian, death is not bad. "Precious in the
sight of the LORD is the death of his saints" (Psalm 116:15).
Death is sad for the Christians who are left behind to live
in this world without our loved ones, but when a Christian
is transported from this world into God's eternal world,
there is rejoicing in heaven. "Thou shalt guide me with thy
counsel, and afterward receive me to glory" (Psalm 73:24).

The Bible also teaches that God controls (in contrast to
"originates") the trouble that comes our way. "But as for
you, ye thought evil against me; but God *meant* [emphasis
mine] it unto good, to bring it to pass, as it is this day, to
save much people alive" (Genesis 50:20).

James 5:11 states: "You have heard of Job's perse-
verance and have seen what the Lord finally brought about.
The Lord is full of compassion and mercy" (NIV). The Living
Bible paraphrase says: "Job is an example of a man who
continued to trust the Lord in sorrow; from his experiences we can see how the Lord's plan finally ended in good,
for he is full of tenderness and mercy."

It may appear that we are victims of our circumstances, but I don't think that is true. In our case, I believe God knew Nate was going to be in an accident, and He chose not to intervene. We are so quick to judge God when He allows some occurrence in our lives that seems negative to us, but we don't take into account all of the times He has protected us and spared us from tragedy. I have observed that Christians have trouble healing from their grief if they don't accept God's sovereignty and acknowledge that God is involved in the lives of His children; He controls the obvious good and the apparent bad that occurs in our lives.

> And the LORD said unto him, Who hath made man's mouth? or who maketh the dumb, or deaf, or the seeing, or the blind? have not I, the LORD?" (Exodus 4:11).

> I know, O LORD, that thy judgments are right, and that thou in faithfulness hast afflicted me. Let, I pray thee, thy merciful kindness be for my comfort, according to thy word unto thy servant (Psalm 119:75,76).

After I appeared on a radio program in December of 1986, I received the following letter from a young man:

> *Several years ago my sister, in her middle twenties, was killed in a car accident. Since then my parents have grown very bitter about God "allowing an innocent, very capable, lovable young woman to die needlessly." They refuse to listen to anything I say about God and believe He couldn't really love them since He took away their child.*
>
> *It's so hard to answer this statement or help them with their bitterness. It is tough for me, too, yet all I can do is believe God has a plan in it all and that nothing is a mistake.*

How we relate to tragedy is our choice. In this letter we see that the parents made one choice and the brother made another. The sibling is working through his grief; the parents are not.

Through suffering we come to know God in all of His greatness, and we come to know ourselves in all of our frailties. We discover we don't have all the answers.

When I was a little girl, my parents and I visited a church in Fort Wayne, Indiana, and I remember a story the pastor told.

When he was young, he and his father would stand out on their front porch and view the stars. As they did, the little boy would recite, "Twinkle, twinkle little star. How I wonder what you are." The stars were a beautiful mystery.

Years passed and the young man went on to college. He listened to the professors as they explained the wonders of the universe. Finally, he looked up at the heavens with an arrogant finger pointed toward the sky and said, "Twinkle, twinkle little star. Now I *know* what you are!" The stars were now simply a fact of science.

As a middle-aged man, one who had experienced the mysteries and complexities of life and who had begun to recognize God's sovereignty over the universe, he looked up at the stars with great humility and stated, "Twinkle, twinkle little star; how I *wonder* what you are."

I have traveled a similar path, from not understanding God at all, to thinking I had Him all figured out, to recognizing that although God has let me in on some of His secrets, there are still many things about life and about Him that I will never understand. But after running the gamut of questions and of feelings, I have come to the conclusion that it is important for me to focus on who God *is* rather than on what He can, will or should do.

When the three Hebrew children were thrown into the fiery furnace, they knew God was capable of rescuing them; however, they did not know if He would choose to show His power in that way.

> Shadrach, Meshach, and Abednego replied, "O Nebuchadnezzar, we are not worried about what will happen to us. If we are thrown into the flaming furnace, our God is able to deliver us; and he will deliver us out of your

hand, Your Majesty. But if he doesn't, please understand, sir, that even then we will never under any circumstance serve your gods or worship the golden statue you have erected" (Daniel 3:16-18, TLB).

They focused on who He was, not on what He would do.

He is the God who created the universe, numbered my days even before I was formed, and loved me enough to die for me. I serve a great God! If things sometimes don't seem to go according to my plan, it's not that God failed or even necessarily that I failed, but simply that I didn't see His plan. God can see the entire plan for my life and my loved ones' lives all in one quick glance, but I only see a little here and a little there.

> "For I know the plans that I have for you," declares the LORD, "plans for welfare and not for calamity to give you a future and a hope" (Jeremiah 29:11, NASB).

In an earlier chapter, I mentioned a lady by the name of Bobbi who found my book, *Roses in December,* just a few months after her daughter's death, at a point when she thought she was losing her mind. Today I received another letter from Bobbi and it is so timely, I must share it with you.

> *I feel I'm making some real progress at last in dealing with Shannon's death. About a month ago I realized that my asking Why? continually was actually hindering my recovery. I was asking more to protest than for any other reason, and in that way I was making it hard for God to use me and heal me. I have a larger sense of God's peace now.*

Suffering comes to all people, but as we surrender to God's power and His sovereignty, He will give us the ability to face our troubles, grow strong through them and use our experiences for His glory. Oswald Chambers points out:

> Suffering is the heritage of the bad, of the penitent, and of the Son of God. Each one ends in the cross. The bad thief is crucified, the penitent thief is crucified, and the Son of God is crucified. By these signs we know the

widespread heritage of suffering.[1]

Suffering truly is a universal experience. Some people choose to sing a song of rebellion, but others sing a song of surrender. Not passive surrender, but the surrender that signifies we have acknowledged there is a power beyond ourselves who cares for us and controls our world. As we bend our knee to that power and sing the song of willing surrender, a supernatural peace will be ours.

A New Song

Where do we go from here?

"He has given me a new song to sing, of praises to our God. Now many will hear of the glorious things he did for me, and stand in awe before the Lord, and put their trust in him" (Psalm 40:3, TLB).

Wherever I go to speak to hurting people, they always ask, "Does it ever get better? When will the pain go away?"

My answer is, "Yes, it can get better. No, the pain does not go away, at least not by itself."

What I've tried to show in this book is that you must face the pain, the fear, the despair, the anger, the stigma, the confusion and the loneliness, and you must make an active decision to turn those negatives into the positives of strength, peace, freedom, power and hope. You can take the old song that was sung in a minor key, and you can transpose it into a harmonious melody. It's your choice. No one can do it for you, but if you're willing to try, Jesus Christ is willing to help you. He has a new song waiting for you.

"O the depth of the riches both of the wisdom and knowledge of God! How unsearchable are his judgments, and his ways past finding out!" (Romans 11:33).

I certainly don't have the answers to why life takes the twists and turns that it does, but I have seen that God can

131

use all those twists and turns for His glory. If you are willing to let Him use your experiences, the opportunities will amaze you.

A few months ago as I was leaving for a trip, I checked my bags at the curb and went into the airport. As I walked in, I began thinking, *You don't have one of your books with you. You need to have a book with you.* Finally, the feeling became so strong that I walked back through the airport, went to the curb baggage check and found my briefcase. I unlocked it, got two copies of my book, relocked my briefcase, and went back into the airport.

Once on the airplane, I was seated next to a man who commented that he wished the weather had been better in California while he was here. I asked, "Are you here on business or vacation?"

The man started to answer, but then he got a very confused look on his face, and his eyes filled with tears. Finally, he said, "I was here to bury my eighteen-year-old son."

I reached into my bag and pulled out a copy of my book as I said, "Sir, I don't know if you believe in divine appointments, but you've just had one."

For the next three hours this man poured out his heart to me — a total stranger. I have learned that death knows no strangers. I realize that since my children's deaths I have become more sensitive to God and to others. Before their deaths I probably would have been too occupied with the busyness of life to even have heard God's voice telling me to go back and get a book, let alone to have responded.

Recently a bereaved parent asked me if I wished I could bring my children back into this world. Of course I would love to have them back; that's an easy decision. But then as I reflected on all I have learned and how I have changed since their deaths, I thought to myself, *I would love to have them back of course, but I would never want to be the*

Marilyn Heavilin I was before they died. I didn't know what life was all about.

Through my children's deaths, I have learned that life is not just about living; it is about caring, loving, hurting and dying. As we walk through these different experiences of living and of dying and sing the songs of December together, we are friends.

I have decided to use this unique bond that I have with fellow sufferers in as positive a way as I can, and that's the challenge I leave with you.

Let the Lord give you a new song—not a song of avoidance where you just bury all of your pain and hurt, but a new song of praises to your God. Let others hear of the glorious things He has done for you so that they can put their trust in Him.

Last Spring after an article about *Roses in December* appeared in our local newspaper, I received a phone call from Jackie. She explained that her twins Ryan and Eric had been born the previous August. The day they were to come home from the hospital, Ryan died of crib death at the hospital, just minutes before Jackie and her husband arrived to take the babies home. I could hear the pain in Jackie's voice as she shared that she was struggling to move past her pain. I got her address and took a book to her that afternoon. Since that time Jackie and I have become good friends, and I was deeply touched when I received the following beautiful poem from her at Christmas.

Dear Marilyn,

If God gives us roses
   So that we might have memories,
Then He must give us friends, like you
   To help us when we grieve.
You are a rose in my bouquet
   That grows larger every day;
Because of you I gain the strength
   To continue on my way.
Because of you I reach out
   As you have done to me—
You set such a fine example
   Of faith and tranquility.
You have met God's many challenges
   With grace and dignity;
You are an inspiration to us all
   Who have been touched by tragedy.
So as this Christmas Day approaches
   And sadness comes to fill your heart,
Please take comfort in your knowing
   How much you've come and been a part—
Of my life, my faith, my future.
   Looking to accept God's will,
Gaining strength, hope, and courage—
   These the things your book instills.
What a tribute to Jimmy, Ethan, Nathan,
   Your three young and precious sons;
How very proud they each must be
   Of their strong and courageous Mom.
That you could stop and take a moment
   To place others' grief before your own—
And write a book to help the many
   Who feel lost and so alone—
Tells us all that your sons live on
   In the heart and soul of you;
That just as they have touched your life,
   So they have touched our sad lives too.
May this thought be your gift
   To your sons this Christmas Day:
That as you touch the lives of many,
   So, too, their love is here to stay.
                        —Jackie Hoar

Sing a new song to the Lord!
Sing it everywhere around the world!
Sing out his praises! Bless his name.
Each day tell someone that he saves.
Publish his glorious acts
throughout the earth.
Tell everyone
about the amazing things he does
(Psalm 96:1-3, TLB).

 *Notes*

CHAPTER 1
1. This quote is generally credited to Sir James Barrie, the author of *Peter Pan.*
2. The Compassionate Friends is an internationally known self-help support group for bereaved parents. For further information, you may write to them at P. O. Box 3696, Oak Brook, IL 60522-3696, phone (312) 990-0010
3. Marilyn Willett Heavilin, *Roses in December* (San Bernardino, CA: Here's Life Publishers, 1987).

CHAPTER 2
1. Florence Littauer, *Personality Plus* (Old Tappan, NJ: Fleming H. Revell, 1983).
2. William R. Dubin, M.D., "Sudden Unexpected Death: Intervention With the Survivors," *Annals of Emergency Medicine* (January 1986), 15:1.
3. Betty Brenner, "Acute grief can cause death, minister says here," *The Flint Journal* (February 25, 1978).

CHAPTER 3
1. Florence Littauer, *Blow Away the Black Clouds* (Eugene, OR: Harvest House Publishers, 1979), pp. 35-50.
2. Philippian Ministries is committed to seeing Christians both spiritually secure and emotionally free. For more information, contact: PHILIPPIAN MINISTRIES, 8515 Greenville Ave., Suite N-203, Dallas, TX 75243, phone (214) 343-8093.
3. Joni Eareckson Tada and Steve Estes, *A Step Further* (Grand Rapids, MI: Zondervan Publishing House, 1978), pp. 15-16.

CHAPTER 5
1. Marilyn Willett Heavilin, *Becoming a Woman of Honor* (San Bernardino, CA: Here's Life Publishers, 1988).

CHAPTER 7
1. Harvey A. Elder, M.D., "Aids and the Family," a seminar held at Loma Linda University, Loma Linda, California, on February 7, 1988.

CHAPTER 8
1. Ann Landers, *The San Bernardino Sun* (March 9, 1986).
2. Darrin R. Lehman, John H. Ellard, and Camille B. Wortman, "Social Support for the Bereaved: Recipients' and Providers' Perspectives on What Is Helpful," *Journal of Consulting and Clinical Psychology* (1986), Volume 54, No. 4, pp. 438-46.

3. Ibid.

CHAPTER 10

1. Darrin R. Lehman, John H. Ellard, and Camille B. Wortman, "Social Support for the Bereaved: Recipients' and Providers' Perspectives on What Is Helpful," *Journal of Consulting and Clinical Psychology* (1986), Volume 54, No. 4, pp. 438-46.
2. Ibid.
3. "Your Grief: You Are Not Going Crazy," published by MADD (April 5, 1984). For more information on this organization, contact: MADD, International Office, P. O. Box 18200, Fort Worth, TX 76118.
4. Lois Duncan, "Funerals Are for the Living," *Woman's Day* (March 4, 1986), p. 120.
5. Ibid.
6. William R. Dubin, M.D., "Sudden Unexpected Death: Intervention With the Survivors," *Annals of Emergency Medicine* (January 1986), 15:1.

CHAPTER 11

1. Pastor John Emmans, *The Furnace of Affliction* (San Bernardino, CA: CBC Publications, May 1971).

CHAPTER 12

1. Harry Verploegh, editor, *Oswald Chambers, The Best From All His Books* (Nashville, TN: Oliver-Nelson Books, 1987), p. 343.